By S. J. Perelman

he

eauty

art

S. J. PERELMAN

Simon and Schuster · New York · 1963

First Printing

LIBRARY OF CONGRESS CATALOG CARD NUMBER: 63–16025
MANUFACTURED IN THE UNITED STATES OF AMERICA
BY THE BOOK PRESS, BRATTLEBORO, VERMONT

THE BEAUTY PART was presented by *Michael Ellis* in association with *Edmund Anderson* at the *Music Box Theatre, New York City, December 26, 1962, with the following cast, listed in order of appearance:*

OCTAVIA WEATHERWAX	Alice Ghostley
MIKE MULROY	David Doyle
MILO LEOTARD ALLARDYCE DUPLESSIS WEATHERWAX	Bert Lahr
LANCE WEATHERWAX	Larry Hagman
SAM FUSSFELD	Bernie West
APRIL MONKHOOD	Patricia Englund
VAN LENNEP	Gil Gardner
HAGEDORN	William Le Massena
BUNCE	David Doyle
VISHNU	Arnold Soboloff
HYACINTH BEDDOES LAFFOON	Bert Lahr
GODDARD QUAGMEYER	Joseph Leon
GLORIA KRUMGOLD	Charlotte Rae
SEYMOUR KRUMGOLD	Bernie West
HARRY HUBRIS	Bert Lahr
ROB ROY FRUITWELL	Sean Garrison
MAURICE BLOUNT	David Doyle
BORIS PICKWICK	William Le Massena
CHENILLE SCHREIBER	Fiddle Viracola
KITTY ENTRAIL	Alice Ghostley
VERNON EQUINOX	Arnold Soboloff
MRS. YOUNGHUSBAND	Charlotte Rae

GRACE FINGERHEAD	Alice Ghostley
CURTIS FINGERHEAD	David Doyle
FISH-MARKET BOY	Gil Gardner
EMMETT STAGG	William Le Massena
WORMSER	Bernie West
NELSON SMEDLEY	Bert Lahr
ROWENA INCHCAPE	Charlotte Rae
RUKEYSER	Arnold Soboloff
WAGNERIAN	David Doyle
SHERRY QUICKLIME	Fiddle Viracola
ELMO	Gil Gardner
HENNEPIN	William Le Massena
POTEAT	Bernie West
CAMERAMAN	Maurice Brenner
HANRATTY	David Doyle
JUDGE HERMAN J. RINDERBRUST	Bert Lahr
BAILIFF	William Le Massena
POLICEMAN	Gil Gardner
ROXANA DE VILBISS	Marie Wallace
JOE GOURIELLI	Arnold Soboloff
MRS. LAFCADIO MIFFLIN	Charlotte Rae

Directed by NOEL WILLMAN
Settings and lighting by WILLIAM PITKIN
Costumes by ALVIN COLT
Incidental music by DON WALKER

Act I

Act II

HARRY HUBRIS

Bert Lahr as...

WING LOO'S FATHER

hotographs

NELSON SMEDLEY

MILO LEOTARD ALLARDYCE
DUPLESSIS WEATHERWAX

Act I SCENE 5

Act I SCENE 3

Act II SCENE 4

Act II SCENE 4

Act II SCENE 5

Act II SCENE 6

ct One

Part One

Act I

SCENE 1

SCENE: *The library of the luxurious Park Avenue triplex of*
MR. *and* MRS. MILO WEATHERWAX. *The decor is posh
Madison Avenue Oriental crossed with Ginsburg and
Levy early American. Constance Spry flower arrange-
ments, a Buddha head, a vase, and two abstract paint-
ings on walls.*

TIME: *Late afternoon.*

AT RISE: *As the stage lights up,* OCTAVIA WEATHERWAX, *a
chic, poised woman in her late thirties paces nervously,
a crumpled handkerchief pressed against her lips.*
MIKE MULROY, *a private eye in the classic Raymond
Chandler tradition, stands nearby consulting a pocket
notebook.*

MULROY: No use being huffy, Mrs. Weatherwax. A private
eye like I—like me, that is—I've got to know which skele-
ton's in what closet.

OCTAVIA: Your line of work makes a man pretty nosy, I
daresay.

MULROY: Look, Mrs. Weatherwax. I've got a dusty office
in the Arbogast Building. My clients pay me a hundred
dollars down as a retainer and ten cents a mile, but that
doesn't entitle them to poke into my psyche.

OCTAVIA: Then we understand each other. Suppose you give me your report.

MULROY: Mr. Weatherwax left the house at 11:14, took a hack to a dairy restaurant on Second Avenue, and had a plate of soup containing *kreplach*. I checked that out with the manager—he lives in the Bath Beach section of Brooklyn. Mr. Weatherwax then made a seven-minute call from a pay phone to a party on the Regent exchange.

OCTAVIA: A woman?

MULROY (*Evasively*): Well, I really don't like to say—

OCTAVIA: See here, Mulroy—I hired you to investigate my husband's extramarital didoes. Let's not be coy.

MULROY: Yes, ma'am.

OCTAVIA: Now, who was she? Who is this person?

MULROY: A television actress, Mrs. Weatherwax.

OCTAVIA: A what?

MULROY: Well, not really an actress. She poses for commercials.

OCTAVIA: What kind?

MULROY: Er—ladies' underthings, I believe.

OCTAVIA: What kind?

MULROY: Gee, Mrs. Weatherwax, does that make any difference?

OCTAVIA: What kind?

MULROY: All right. Brassieres.

OCTAVIA: I deserve it for asking. How old is she?

MULROY: She's no chicken—at least twenty-three. A very ordinary girl—long legs—tiny waist. Her lips are too lush —kind of ripples when she walks—

OCTAVIA: What does?

MULROY: Her hair. It's chestnut and she wears it loose— cascading down her shoulders—and when she laughs—

OCTAVIA (*Sharply*): That'll do, Mulroy. You needn't launch into a rhapsody.

MULROY: Yes, ma'am.

OCTAVIA: This apartment you spoke of is where?

MULROY: East 73rd, between Park and Lex. Modified French Provincial furniture with mirror accents and white wall-to-wall carpeting. Foam chairs in fake zebra and a coffee table made out of an old set of bellows. (*Refers to notes*) The bedroom is done in pink, with ruffles—

OCTAVIA: Never mind. I can visualize it.

MULROY: I'm sorry, I realize what a shock it always is. I haven't been a private snoop nine years for nothing.

OCTAVIA: Thank you. Nice of you to empathize.

MULROY: Mrs. Weatherwax, I'm not very good at putting my thoughts into words.

OCTAVIA: Say it in your own way.

MULROY: May I kiss you?

OCTAVIA: If you like. (THEY *embrace.* SHE *turns, his arms around her*) Oh, Mulroy, what's to become of us?

MULROY: I don't know—I don't care. All I know is that you've spoiled me for other girls.

OCTAVIA: I felt that in my heart's deep core.

MULROY: Octavia—

OCTAVIA (*Recoils from him*): You knew my first name all along.

MULROY (*Sheepishly*): Maybe I overstepped.

OCTAVIA: You have. I'm one of the richest women in America, Mulroy. A mere nod from me creates a convulsion in Wall Street. My son, Lance, is Skull and Bones at Yale. It's time for you to leave the room.

MULROY: Yes, ma'am. (*Retrieves hat, points to vase on stand*) My, that's lovely. Genuine Sèvres, isn't it?

OCTAVIA: Yes. How did you know?

MULROY: Oh, I dabble in porcelain a bit.

OCTAVIA: Isn't that strange? I rather sensed you had a flair.

MULROY: I haven't been a private snoop twelve years for nothing.

OCTAVIA: It was nine last time.

MULROY (*Kneels impetuously at her feet*): It seemed like twelve till you came along.

OCTAVIA: That will be sufficient, Mr. Mulroy.

MULROY (*Chagrined*): Yes, I'd better get back and relieve my partner, Costello. He's on the fire escape outside her flat.

OCTAVIA: Yes, you'd better.

MULROY: You ought to meet that Costello—he's the talented one. He's been exhibited at the Guggenheim.

OCTAVIA: Oh?

MULROY: He does these collages out of seawood and graham crackers.

(*Offstage feminine squeals*)

OCTAVIA: It's Milo. He's home.

MULROY: Hasta luego.

(MILO WEATHERWAX *backs on, obviously detaching himself with difficulty from some fair one.* HE *is a dapper figure in morning coat, pencil-striped trousers.* HE *starts guiltily at the sight of* OCTAVIA)

MILO: Now, look here, Octavia, I just had to give our French maid a severe dressing down.

OCTAVIA: So I heard.

MILO: There's loose rubies all over the foyer. A person could break their ankle! What are we living in, a pigpen?

(*Opens one of the abstract paintings at rear to reveal a bar concealed within*)

OCTAVIA: How was your board meeting, dear?

MILO: Meeting? Why—er—(*Busies himself with glasses*) I didn't attend. I had other fish to fry.

OCTAVIA: Yes, and they crackled, didn't they? (SHE *rises wrathfully*) Milo, this is the handwriting on the wall. Our marriage is washed up—napoo—ausgespielt.

MILO: You're trying to tell me something.

OCTAVIA: I mean that I'm restless, unhappy, bored, and you are, too.

MILO: Maybe you're right. I'll admit I've been chafing at the bit a bit.

OCTAVIA: Ah, well, the fat's in the fire. How are we to break the news to Lance?

MILO: What Lance is that?

OCTAVIA: Why, our twenty-year-old son, which he's home from Yale on his midyears and don't suspicion his folks are rifting.

MILO: Of course, of course. (*With an incredulous head-shake*) Reached man's estate already, has he? Where is our cub at the present writing?

OCTAVIA: In the tack room, furbishing up the accoutrements of his polo ponies.

MILO (*Acidly*): Far better to be furbishing up on his Euclid, lest he drag the name of Weatherwax through the scholastic mire.

LANCE (*Exuberantly, offstage*): Dads! Mums!

OCTAVIA: Shush! Here he comes now. (*Exiting*) You had best handle this. I'm laying down on my chaise lounge with a vinegar compress.

(LANCE, *a handsome youth in jodhpurs, bursts on, looks about inquiringly*)

LANCE: Hi, Dads! Where's Mums?

MILO: Son, we're facing a family crisis and, as per usual, your mother's chickened out.

LANCE: I don't dig you, Guv.

MILO: My boy, the Weatherwax union has blown a gasket.

LANCE: You've lost me, Dads.

MILO: To employ the vulgate, your mother and I have split out.

LANCE (*Sobered*): Rum go, Dads.

MILO: Yes, it's hard on us oldsters, but it isn't going to be easy for you either.

LANCE (*Frightened*): You mean I've got to go to work?

MILO: Don't be asinine! Not as long as there's a penny of your mother's money left.

LANCE: Look, Pater, I . . . that is, me . . . aw, jeepers, can I ask you something man to man?

MILO: Lance, a chap with a sympathetic sire don't have to beat about the bush.

LANCE: Thanks, Pop. Well, I've been running with a pretty serious crowd up at New Haven—lots of bull sessions about *Lolita* and Oscar Wilde.

MILO: That's the stuff to cut your eyeteeth on, son. A fellow has to learn to crawl before he can walk.

LANCE: Reet. (*Brows knit perplexedly*) And I've been wondering more and more of late. Where does our money come from?

MILO (*Evasively*): Why—er—the doctor brings it. In a little black bag.

LANCE: Aw, gee, Dad, I'm old enough to know. *Please.*

MILO: My, you children grow up quick nowadays. (*Fatalistically*) Very well. Have you ever heard of the Weatherwax All-Weather Garbage Disposal Plan?

LANCE: You—you mean whereby garbage is disposed of in all weathers by having neatly uniformed attendants call for and remove it?

MILO: Yes. That is the genesis of our scratch.

LANCE (*As the realization sinks home*): Oh, sir, I want to die!

MILO: Steady on, lad. After all, think of the millions which, were it not for our kindly ministrations, their homes would be a welter of chicken bones, fruit peels, and rancid yoghurt.

LANCE: I'll never be able to hold up my head in Bulldog circles again.

MILO: Nonsense, lad. Why, you wear the keenest threads on the campus and you're *persona grata* to myriad Eli frats.

LANCE: No. Father, this is the end of halcyon days in the groves of Academe. I'm going away.

MILO: Going away? Where? Why?

LANCE: Dad—it isn't only your revelation that turned my world topsy-turvy. There's another reason I've got to prove myself. I've fallen in love with a wonderful person.

MILO: Hm-m-m, I thought there was a colored gentleman in the woodpile.

LANCE: No, this is a girl, Dad. I met her last Christmas in Greenwich Village.

MILO: Well, you mustn't fling your cap over the moon. Remember, an apple knocker like you could easily fall into the hands of an adventuress.

LANCE (*Hotly*): Adventuress? April Monkhood's the most sincere human being who ever lived!

MILO: April Monkhood . . . ? I didn't quite catch that name.

LANCE: She's a designer.

MILO: It figures.

LANCE: You'd love her, sir, honest you would. She's spiritual —vibrant—artistic to the nth degree. April awoke something in me I never knew existed—a thirst for beauty. I've got to express it somehow—in words or paint or music.

MILO: I know, my boy, I know. I had the same creative urge when I was your age.

LANCE: What became of it?

MILO: I sublimated it. Nowadays I sponsor a few gifted individuals on the side—sopranos, exotic dancers—

LANCE: Each of us has to work out their own salvation, Dad. What was yours?

MILO: Sex, and plenty of it.

LANCE: Mine's in the arts somewhere, in what branch I can't say until I try them all. But I'm not going to compromise. April's never compromised, and if I'm going to be worthy of her, I've got to hew to my resolve.

MILO (*Shrugs, extracts envelope*): Very well, then. Before you start, I want you to have this keepsake.

LANCE: Gee, Dads.

MILO: It won't buy much except dreams, but it's been in the family for generations.

LANCE: What is it?

MILO: A letter of credit.

LANCE: I can't take it, sir. To me it's like tainted.

MILO: Great Scott, lad, you can't walk out of here empty-handed. You'll need money, introductions, shelter—

LANCE: No, Dad.

MILO: But I won't let you sleep in the street! There's our old railroad car underneath the Waldorf-Astoria. Take it—it's only using up steam.

LANCE (*Simply*): I'm sorry, Dad. From now on, I walk alone.

(HE *exits.* OCTAVIA *enters, looks nonplused after him*)

OCTAVIA: Why, goodness, whatever ails the child? Milo, my woman's intuition tells me you've just had a stormy colloquy with Lance.

MILO: What Lance is that?

OCTAVIA: Why, our twenty-two-year-old son, which he's home from Yale on his midyears and don't suspicion his folks are rifting.

MILO: Oh, yes, of course. Well, if you need me, I'm laying down on my chaise lounge with a vinegar compress.
    HE *exits*)

OCTAVIA (*Ruefully*): Incorrigible boy! I sometimes wonder where it will all end.

(As SHE throws up her hands à la ZaSu Pitts and drifts off, scenery revolves to—)

Act I

SCENE 2

SCENE: APRIL MONKHOOD's apartment. A standard Village locale such as is occupied by any young career woman, but recently redecorated to express the personality of the occupant. Fishnet looped around walls, interspersed with glass spheres. Two or three score notary seals, both gold and red, pasted indiscriminately on window shades, drapes and sofa. A profusion of fake leopardskin upholstery, fake Negro sculpture and corresponding claptrap of the sort found along East 8th Street.

TIME: Two days later.

AT RISE: APRIL MONKHOOD, an attractive girl in her early twenties given to self-dramatization and endowed with magnificent secondary sexual characteristics and practically no sense of humor, is mounted on a small aluminum stepladder, attaching a pot of ferns to a bracket. FUSSFELD, a telephone repairman, stands nearby at an end table, talking into phone.

FUSSFELD: Checking Algonquin 4-1014 . . . (Phone rings) Loud and clear. (Hangs up, addresses APRIL as HE reassembles kit) Well, you're O.K. now, Miss Monkhood.

APRIL: Thank heavens—I was on the brink of suicide. Absolutely bereft! I get so many calls in my business I couldn't exist without a second phone.

FUSSFELD: Oh? What line you in, may I ask?

APRIL: Well, several, but chiefly jewelry design. Abstract things—you know, conversation pieces.

FUSSFELD: You don't say.

APRIL: I handle just a few connoisseurs. If someone comes to me—say, a cynic with an appetite for subtle blasphemies —or a woman in a black gown with a sense of what's stark and dramatic—or a man whose id cries out for a massive and tortured ring—I distill their personality.

FUSSFELD: I pegged you for some artistic field when I walked in your place.

APRIL: Yes, I've been redecorating. Of course, it's incomplete as yet.

(*Looks about worriedly*)

FUSSFELD: I'd sprinkle a couple of magazines around, or maybe a dish of cashews. They're tasty and they help soak up the humidity.

APRIL: No, no, what it really yearns for is a great splendid tree right over there. I've ordered a Bechtel's flowering crab.

FUSSFELD: A tree? Wouldn't the landlord raise the roof?

APRIL (*Sunnily*): Oh, yes, he promised he would. (*Sound of door buzzer off*) Would you just let in whoever that is on your way?

FUSSFELD: Sure. G'bye.

(HE *exits*)

LANCE (*Off*): April! April!

APRIL (*As HE enters*): Lance Weatherwax! Whatever in the world are you doing here?

LANCE (*Tensely*): April—I've got to talk to you. Right away.

APRIL: Of course, dear. Come in . . . (*With concern*) You look so distrait. Has something happened?

LANCE: Well, yes—kind of. I bet I've walked fifty miles the past couple of days, trying to think things through.

APRIL: You must have been in real travail.

LANCE: I was.

APRIL: You poor boy.

LANCE (*Reacts to décor for first time*): What—what's going on here?

APRIL: I've had it done over. Isn't it delectable?

LANCE: Oh, great. I mean, it like hits you right in the eye.

APRIL: Does it say anything to you? You don't feel it's overdone?

LANCE: Overdone? It's underdone! You couldn't omit one detail without damaging the—the entire concept.

APRIL (*Hugs him*): You old sorcerer. You know just the words to thaw a woman's heart. (SHE *kisses him*) Let's have a drink to celebrate. Sit ye doon (LANCE *sits couch*) —and I'll open a bottle of Old Rabbinical. (*Pushes him backward on studio couch and whisks bottle from cabinet, from which SHE proceeds to fill two glasses. The phone rings; SHE answers hurriedly*) Yes? . . . Who? . . . Oh, hi! . . . No, I can't. I have people here . . . What? No, I have to wash my hair . . . Yes, silly . . . Why don't you do that? I'm always here . . . 'Bye. (*Hangs up*) Really, some men are just impossible. They think all they have to do is whistle.

LANCE: Who was that?

APRIL: My ex-fiancé, of all people.

LANCE: Hanh? You never told me you'd been engaged.

APRIL: Oh, Sensualdo and I haven't seen each other in ages. He's a monster—an absolute fiend.

LANCE: Sensualdo? His name sounds Mexican.

APRIL: Uh-uh—Peruvian. One of those insanely jealous types. Tried to stab a man I was having a Coke with. That's what broke up our engagement.

LANCE: Is he—er—back there now?

APRIL: In Peruvia? Well, he shuttles between there and Staten Island. Something to do with vicuñas or emeralds— I really don't know.

LANCE (*Urgently*): April, there's something very important I—

APRIL: As a matter of fact, he was a prince compared to my first fiancé. Did you ever hear of Benno Vontz, the sculptor?

LANCE: No, I can't say I have, but—

APRIL: Benno designed that abstract saddle on top of Neiman-Marcus's in Dallas. A brilliant boy, but terribly neurotic. He used to wake me up in the middle of the day, claiming I'd had affairs with all kinds of people—osteopaths, carhops, bakers. It was a nightmare, my dear—an absolute *cauchemar*. I was practically on the verge of a neuresthenia when I met Ricky.

LANCE: Ricky?

APRIL: He was an auctioneer I met in Atlantic City. Naturally, one thing led to another.

LANCE: And you got engaged.

APRIL: No! Benno found out! One night Ricky and I were driving home in a downpour and his brakes overheated near Asbury Park and we had to take refuge in a motel. Next thing we knew, Benno was all over us with flashbulbs. (*A tragic Mrs. Malaprop*) My dear, it was too sorbid.

LANCE (*Takes her hand*): You poor kid. It's a wonder to me you could live through so much and still remain gay and *joie de vivre*.

APRIL: That's because I sublimate myself in my work, Lance. Whenever life gets frantic, why, I rush to my bench and fashion a brooch or earrings that crystallize a dewdrop of ecstasy. Your great craftsmen have always done that, right back to Cellini.

LANCE: April, if you only knew how your eyes light up when you talk about art.

APRIL (*Languorously*): Do they?

LANCE: There's a kind of a glow in them. They're like mysterious violet pools, full of understanding . . . and wisdom . . . and—oh, terrific tolerance. Not like those empty-headed little debs I used to date before I met you.

APRIL: Why, Lance, I've never heard you so articulate before. It's as if you'd been freed, somehow.

LANCE (*Vehemently*): I have. I've come to a very important decision about my future, April. I have to know right away how you feel.

APRIL (*Placing finger on his lips*): Please, Lance, for both our sakes—don't say anything you might regret.

LANCE: No, no—I've got to. You see, this door suddenly opened in my mind and I realized what truly matters to me.

APRIL (*Tempest-tossed*): Oh, Lance, do you know what you're saying?

LANCE: Yes, yes, I do. April, I've decided to become a writer.

APRIL: You *what?*

LANCE: Or maybe a painter.

APRIL (*Barely suppressed irritation*): Oh, Lance, don't be an Airedale.

LANCE (*Wounded*): What's the matter? Don't you think I have the ability?

APRIL: Er—of course, but—well, I was just a little overwhelmed. I mean, it's such a tremendous challenge.

LANCE: I want to accept that challenge—I want to unleash whatever creative powers there are inside me. But my problem is—how do I become a writer?

APRIL: Buy a magazine—or maybe a chain of them. I understand the *Saturday Evening Post* is up for grabs—

LANCE: No, siree, I won't be a lousy dilettante. I'm going to start humbly, get the smell of printer's ink . . .

APRIL (*Lighting up*): Wait—wait! Eureka!

LANCE: I beg your pardon?

APRIL: What a blind little fool I've been! The perfect way to express yourself—it's right in front of you!

LANCE: I don't follow.

APRIL: Let's plunge into the depths together! Scale the heights together!

LANCE: How?

APRIL: Well, you know what a disorganized scatterbrain I am away from my workbench—I haven't a clue to facts or figures. I need someone with divine good taste to counsel me—someone whose judgment I respect.

LANCE: But where would I contribute my creative talent?

APRIL: Why, in a hundred ways . . . Right here, for example—(*Extracts crumpled paper from blouse*)—this came in the morning mail. What does it mean?

LANCE: It's from the bank. It says they're returning your check for $471 due to insufficient funds.

APRIL: It must be that consignment of turquoise nutpicks I ordered from Santa Fe. Those Navajos are so grasping . . . What should I do about it?

LANCE: You must put the money in the bank to cover the overdraft.

APRIL (*Triumphantly*): There—you see how much more practical you are than I? Very well—you handle it, love.

LANCE: How do you mean?

APRIL: Why, when you leave here, just drop by the Centerboard National and deposit that amount, until I get straightened out.

LANCE: But I haven't any money.

APRIL: Of course, how dense of me. Nobody carries that much around. Well, here's a thought—ring up your father's accountant and tell him to deposit it.

LANCE. I don't think you understand, April. I've cut myself off. I've broken with my family.

APRIL: But you haven't broken with your accountant, surely.

LANCE: With everybody.

APRIL: You're teasing.

LANCE (*Exhibiting a few coins*): This is all the money I have.

APRIL (*Instantly*): Lance, I don't think we're quite ready to work together. Obey your original impulse—go and get the smell of printer's ink. Go see Hyacinth Beddoes Laffoon right away.

LANCE: Who is she?

APRIL: The woman who publishes all those magazines— *Gory Story*—*Sanguinary Love*—*Spicy Mortician*.

LANCE: But they're just pulp fiction, full of blood and thunder . . .

APRIL: My dear Lance, wake up. Some of our most enduring American authors come out of that milieu.

LANCE (*Fired*): Maybe you're right, April. Maybe I ought to contact her.

APRIL: Without further ado! Now, you buzz right over to Laffoon House and storm the redoubts. I'd help you storm except I have to rush out to an appointment.

LANCE (*As* SHE *turns away*): When am I going to see you again?

APRIL: Quién sabe, corazón? (*A sudden inspiration*) I'll tell you what—why don't you drop in at my housewarming next Tuesday? And dig up an itty-bitty case of Scotch on the way, will you? There's a dear. (*Pushes him out, turns*

back into room. Phone rings; SHE *answers brusquely*) Yes?
. . . Who? . . . Oh, it's you again. Now listen, Sensualdo,
I told you, no monkey business—what? What new emeralds? (*Second phone rings*) Look—hold on just one
minute—(*Snatches up other receiver*) Hello? Who? . . .
Well, stranger! . . . Of course I have, Benno darling—absolutely heartsick . . . No—no, I couldn't . . . Anselmo
who? . . . Olivetti? Not the *typewriter* Olivettis . . . Honey,
wait one second, my other phone . . . (*Clasps phone to
her, jabbers into the other*) Look, Sensualdo, I just stepped
out of my shower and I'm holding a big bag of groceries.
Why don't we meet at the Drake about midnight and
you bring along the adding machines . . . I mean the
emeralds . . .

(*The scenery has been moving during end of speech,
and now revolves to—*)

Act I

SCENE 3

SCENE: Office of HYACINTH BEDDOES LAFFOON. A chamber devoid of furniture and of uncompromising severity, with only enough indications to stamp it as a publisher's sanctum. The walls display a couple of lurid pulp magazine covers with violent themes and broad mammary exposure.

TIME: A week later.

AT RISE: BUNCE, VAN LENNEP, HAGEDORN and VISHNU, four typical crew-haired and brainwashed editorial assistants, Christmas tigers all, are grouped in a corner. THEY wear identical blazers with breast patches exhibiting the letter "L," and buzz between themselves as THEY look over at LANCE isolated across the room.

VAN LENNEP: When did you hear about it?

HAGEDORN: I didn't. When I arrived this morning, there was a strange polo coat in my locker.

BUNCE (Worriedly): I was told not one word by Mrs. Hyacinth Beddoes Laffoon about a new editorial assistant.

VAN LENNEP: Nor me. She usually gives me an intimation—if only a wink—

HAGEDORN: She kind of winked at me at yesterday's meeting.

VAN LENNEP (*Superior*): No, I saw that. It was a belch.

VISHNU: That's right. She took a spoon of bicarb right after.

BUNCE: Besides, which magazine's got a vacancy? We're full up.

VAN LENNEP: He might be taking over that gland column— "You and Your Gonads."

VISHNU: Say, you don't suppose it's the doctor she spoke of?

HAGEDORN: What one?

VISHNU: She said we all needed a good proctologist.

VAN LENNEP: Cheese it! Here she comes now!

> (*With the silken smoothness of a Cadillac, an executive desk glides in, behind it* HYACINTH BEDDOES LAFFOON. *She is the epitome of female editors, chic, sleek, and murderous. Desktop holds a neat stack of magazines, dictagraph*)

HYACINTH: Good morning. (*Cordially*) How are you, Weatherwax?

LANCE: Fine, Mrs. Laffoon.

HYACINTH: Men, I want you to welcome a new member to our editorial family—Mr. Lance Weatherwax.

> (*Ad lib greetings; the staff bestow saccharine smiles as* THEY *scan* LANCE)

BUNCE (*Delicately*): Er—how would you describe Mr. Weatherwax, Chief? Is he a writer?

HYACINTH (*Coldly*): I don't believe in labels, Bunce. When I smell a fresh, original talent in the marketplace, I buy it. This young man is going to be a dynamic addition to our team. All right, now, drain the sludge out of your think-tanks. We're going to brainstorm. (*Chattering sound*) What's that chattering sound?

BUNCE (*Eagerly*): It's Hagedorn's teeth, Mrs. Laffoon. I've been meaning to squeal on him. Gosh, you ought to hear the noise he makes over the partition! A man can hardly concentrate.

HYACINTH: Oh, you have trouble concentrating, do you?

BUNCE: No, no—it'd take a lot more than that to upset *me!* I could work in a boiler factory!

HYACINTH: You may yet. Meanwhile, Hagedorn, let's have those choppers out before our next conference.

HAGEDORN: I'll see my extractionist in the lunch hour, Chief.

HYACINTH: Well, see that you do! Now, then, I've had my ear to the ground lately and I get a very . . . strange . . . impression. Some of you disagree with the policy of my new magazine, *Shroud*.

VAN LENNEP: Hell's bells, Hyacinth! Where'd you ever pick up that crazy idea?

HYACINTH: From the dictaphone I had installed in the water cooler. Does this sound familiar, Van Lennep? (*Reads* from flimsy) "Just give the old windbag enough rope. You'll see, the public'll pin her ears back."

VAN LENNEP (*Squirming*): I—I was referring to Miss Lovibond, who solicits those ads for lost manhood. You said yourself the magazine needed more chic.

HYACINTH: Well, you squirmed out of that one all right, but watch your step. I'm sentimental enough to think this organization can't function without one-hundred-percent loyalty.

VISHNU: And you've got it, Mrs. Laffoon.

BUNCE: Why, we venerate the ground you walk on!

VAN LENNEP: Right down the line.

HAGEDORN: I'll say, Chief.

HYACINTH: At the same time, no ass-kissing! I want honest, sturdy, independent reactions—is that clear?

BUNCE: Like crystal!

HAGEDORN: Boy, I wish I could express myself so forcefully!

VAN LENNEP: She really cuts it, doesn't she?

VISHNU: What an editor!

HYACINTH: O.K. Well, I've just had a couple of skull-busters that I'd like to try out on you. First, these covers we've been running. Look at this one—who's responsible for this? A naked girl tied to a bedpost and a chimpanzee brandishing a whip. No more punch than a seed catalogue!

VAN LENNEP: I see the structural weakness.

BUNCE: Demands too much of the reader.

HYACINTH: Correct. We've got to drill him right between the eyes. Now, I visualize a cover with a real revolver barrel pointing at you.

OMNES: Hey . . . Hey . . . Hey . . . Hey . . . Hey . . .

HYACINTH: And a wisp of smoke curling out. The smoke would be engendered in a mechanism hinged to the back cover.

OMNES: Hey! Hey! Hey! Hey! Hey! Hey! Hey! Hey!

LANCE: But Mrs. Laffoon, wouldn't it be kind of bulky?

HYACINTH: Yes, and we could run afoul of the Sullivan Law.

VAN LENNEP: Nah, that can all be worked out!

HAGEDORN: Baby, what an inspiration!

VISHNU: It'll knock Publishers' Row right back on their heels!

BUNCE: Hyacinth, I don't say these things lightly. This idea's got undertow!

VAN LENNEP: I can almost hear those dimes and nickels showering down!

HYACINTH: You bet you can. It's the cashier counting your severance pay. So long, Van Lennep. *Saranoya!* (As HE exits *chopfallen*) There's no room at the top for a yes-man. Good thinking, Weatherwax. As of today, you take over

Van Lennep's duties. You can wear his blazer till yours comes through.

LANCE: Gee, thanks, Mrs. Laffoon.

HYACINTH: Now, let's see how my next idea appeals. What about a country-wide golem contest?

VISHNU: Could you clarify that a bit for us, Chief?

HYACINTH: A competition among our teen-age readers for the best Frankenstein monster built in a home workshop ... How does that lay on the stomach, Bunce?

BUNCE: It stirs me and yet it leaves me cold.

HAGEDORN: I want to throw my arms around it, but something holds me back.

VISHNU: It's as broad as it is long.

BUNCE: How do you—

VISHNU:—feel about it—

HAGEDORN: —yourself?

HYACINTH (*Simpers*): It's my idea.

VISHNU: And you can afford to crow. I know I'd be proud of it!

HYACINTH: Well, I'm not. It's a *bomb.* (*Significantly*) Vishnu, I wish you'd reconsider leaving us. We need you here.

VISHNU: And I feel there's a place for me.

HYACINTH: Not right here, but in the stockroom. Scout around; find an opening—(VISHNU exits)—and clean it. *Arrivaducci!* (As VISHNU exits) By the bye, Weatherwax, I didn't catch your reaction to my idea just now.

LANCE: What idea?

HYACINTH: Ho-ho, that's foxy of you—very good! Pretending you didn't hear it! You've got real executive stature, lad.

LANCE: Gee, thanks.

HYACINTH: Nothing at all. Now, leave me, all of you—run along. You stay, Weatherwax.

BUNCE: But you might need us, boss.

HYACINTH: Go . . . go . . . go!

HAGEDORN (*Spitefully*): Oh, *he's* the palace favorite now, is he?

(BUNCE and HAGEDORN retire, casting black glances at LANCE. HYACINTH has withdrawn lacy handkerchief which SHE presses to her lips in anguish)

HYACINTH: Oh, the jealousies, the intrigues . . . (*Shoulders heaving*) Oh, it's too much. It's insupportable.

LANCE: What is?

HYACINTH: I feel so alone, so inadequate. I'm only a woman in a man's world, trying to cope.

LANCE: But you're on top—I mean, you're in charge. What you say goes.

HYACINTH (*Emotionally*): Do you think that way lies true happiness, Weatherwax? Under this artificial exterior there's a helpless creature that wants to be dominated—to be adored . . .

LANCE: Everybody loves you, Mrs. Laffoon. Honest they do.

HYACINTH: No, no—you're all toadies, parasites. There's not a single living thing I can rely on. Not even a dog.

LANCE (*Fervently*): You could depend on me. Just try.

HYACINTH (*Blinking at him through unshed tears*): You mean it?

LANCE: Oh, I do! Really I do!

HYACINTH: Oh, how wonderful to hear those words! . . . (*Seating herself on desktop*) Weatherwax, as I sit here, I suddenly have a vision. I see a vast publishing enterprise, with the two of us at the helm. Not one of those cockamamie affairs that Henry Luce runs, but a far-flung empire embracing every printed word. (*Buzzer sounds.* SHE *flips switch—a raucous, unidentifiable bark*) Hello! The who? . . . The Weatherwax Trust & Loan Co.? Good—put them on . . . (*Grabs phone, sugar and spice*) Well, are we getting that little half-a-million loan for *Shroud* Magazine? (*Her face clouds over*) Oh, we're not!

(*Cradles phone, outraged*)

LANCE: You were saying . . .

HYACINTH: That you're clean and straight and fine, and I say to you—get out before it's too late.

LANCE: But I only started this morn—

HYACINTH (*Rising*): Are you getting out, or do I have to have you thrown out?

LANCE: Er—yes, ma'am—I only thought . . .

HYACINTH: Hit the road! (HE *exits, confused.* HYACINTH *resumes seat, picks up documents and glares after him. With a snort*) He only thought. That's the trouble with the world nowadays . . . too much thinking. (SHE *flips dictagraph switch*) Lorna? Get me Barry Goldwater.

(*The desk begins moving as* SHE *utters the foregoing, and we revolve into*—)

Act I

SCENE 4

SCENE: GODDARD QUAGMEYER's studio, Greenwich Village. *The studio of a professional painter, devoid of any hint of dilettantism. Skylight at rear facing into street. At center an easel with a partially complete abstract painting, beside it a taboret laden with pigment, fixative bomb, etc. At rear also, an antique Greek plaster cast of a head, tableful of sketch pads, jars of brushes, pencils, dividers, maulstick. A disordered cot dimly in evidence in background.*

TIME: *Morning, several days later.*

AT RISE: *The studio is empty of human life. Then a key is heard in the lock and* GODDARD QUAGMEYER *enters carrying a paper bag. He proceeds to sip coffee from a container he extracts from bag, nibbling on a Danish butterhorn and intently considering the painting on easel.*
He has picked up palette and begun work on canvas when a knock sounds at door. QUAGMEYER *reacts with irritation, attempts to continue. Another couple of knocks, more insistent.*

QUAGMEYER (*Calls off, attention glued to canvas*): Go 'way —nobody's home! (*Another knock;* HE *half-turns*) Quiet

—we're recording! (*Repeated knock;* HE *shouts*) Stop that, will you? Someone's dead here!

(*Still another knock.* QUAGMEYER *ignores it;* LANCE *enters tentatively*)

LANCE: Mr. Quagmeyer?

QUAGMEYER: Yes. What is it?

LANCE: You probably don't recall me.

QUAGMEYER: Your intuition is faultless.

LANCE: I'd like to talk to you if I could.

QUAGMEYER: Well, you can't. I've got a gouache to finish and it's drying on me.

LANCE: My name is Weatherwax. I'm not trying to sell anything.

QUAGMEYER: But *I* am.

LANCE: Lance Weatherwax. My mother owns two of your paintings.

QUAGMEYER (*Reacting*): Oh? . . . Yes, that's right—she does. And as I remember, she paid a tidy little sum for them.

LANCE: Mr. Quagmeyer, how can a person like me tell whether they really have the creative spark?

QUAGMEYER: If it sets fire to your pants.

LANCE: Oh, I know how naïve it sounds—me, Lance Weatherwax, aspiring to the arts.

QUAGMEYER: You've got plenty of company. Every housewife in the country's got a novel under her apron.

LANCE: No, I'm more interested in the visual—

QUAGMEYER: And the dentists are even worse. Do you realize there are twice as many dentists painting in their spare time as there are painters practicing dentistry?

LANCE: I have to fulfill myself, Mr. Quagmeyer.

QUAGMEYER: All over this tremendous country, millions of poor worn-out bastards are *schlepping* home to frozen casseroles because their wives are out studying psycho-ceramics.

LANCE: If I could like write the perfect sonnet or paint one masterpiece, I'd die happy.

QUAGMEYER: Well, you'll never die of starvation, that's one comfort. Your folks have more bread than the Sheik of Kuwait.

LANCE (*With spirit*): They can keep it. The whole six hundred million.

QUAGMEYER: Look, headstrong boy, even Lorenzo de' Medici and Huntington Hartford didn't go that far . . . But, tell me, what do you want from me?

LANCE: Mr. Quagmeyer, from the little you've seen of me, do I have the raw material to be a painter?

QUAGMEYER: Sonny, I'm pressed for time, so you'll excuse me for being blunt. Lay off the Muses—it's a very tough dollar.

LANCE: It's not the financial rewards I'm striving for, sir, it's self-realization! Like Gauguin was searching for when he went to the South Seas.

QUAGMEYER: Oh. Well, in that case, you might have to do the same thing.

LANCE: Do you mean it? Do you think maybe I ought to lose myself in some place like Tahiti—live like the natives do?

QUAGMEYER: Yes, but easy on the poontang.

MRS. KRUMGOLD (*Offstage*): Do me one favor, Seymour, and shut up!

(GLORIA and SEYMOUR KRUMGOLD, *a pair of prosperous Jerseyites, straggle on*)

MR. KRUMGOLD: Last stop! Last stop! You said that an hour ago at the place we bought the Siamese fighting fish.

MRS. KRUMGOLD: Oblige me once in your life and button your lip!

MR. KRUMGOLD: Now you drag me down to Greenwich Village and make me climb five flights of stairs. Me with my duodenal. (MRS. KRUMGOLD *sneers*) You can laugh. Laugh! I was so tensed up last night, I could hardly hold my pinochle hand.

MRS. KRUMGOLD: That'd be a tragedy, all right!

QUAGMEYER: Excuse me.

MRS. KRUMGOLD: Don't interrupt, please!

MR. KRUMGOLD: You'd like to see me keel over, wouldn't you? Any woman that sits around the house studying her husband's insurance policy!

MRS. KRUMGOLD: I resent that deeply!

QUAGMEYER: I beg your pardon.

MRS. KRUMGOLD: You keep out of this!

MR. KRUMGOLD: I wouldn't put it past you to hire assassins.

MRS. KRUMGOLD: You're paranoid!

MR. KRUMGOLD: What about those two truck drivers that stopped me for a light just now? The one wearing mascara looked like a tough customer.

MRS. KRUMGOLD: Those were Bennington girls.

MR. KRUMGOLD: I'm glad I don't have your dirty mind!

MRS. KRUMGOLD: Oh, shut up! (*To* QUAGMEYER, *sweetly*) I'm terribly sorry we're late. Seymour was trapped with his tax consultant.

MR. KRUMGOLD: That lousy crook!

QUAGMEYER: I think you've made a mistake, lady.

MRS. KRUMGOLD: Aren't you Goddard Quagmeyer? I'm Zimmy Vetlugin's cousin. He's your art dealer, isn't he?

QUAGMEYER: Yes.

MRS. KRUMGOLD: Well, I'm Gloria Krumgold. We're here about the painting.

QUAGMEYER: Oh—oh—of course. Now, which canvas was it? It's slipped my mind.

MRS. KRUMGOLD: That Zimmy. I can see he didn't tell you anything.

MR. KRUMGOLD: Gloria, for God's sake—

MRS. KRUMGOLD: Seymour!

QUAGMEYER: Perfectly all right, Mrs. Krumgold. What sort of thing are you looking for?

MRS. KRUMGOLD: We have a special problem—I better describe it. You see, Seymour and I have just built a very lovely home in Passaic Hills. The last word in modrun, except for the stables.

QUAGMEYER: Sounds very attractive.

MRS. KRUMGOLD: We need something for the living room. The idea is, in the center there's a sunken conversation pit.

QUAGMEYER: Sounds dangerous.

MRS. KRUMGOLD: But that's not our problem. It's the free-standing fireplace in the middle. We need a picture that would be suitable.

QUAGMEYER: To do what?

MRS. KRUMGOLD (*Gestures*): To go around it.

QUAGMEYER: I don't paint round pictures.

MRS. KRUMGOLD (*Patiently*): Canvas wouldn't work, naturally, on a fireplace, so we thought maybe you would do it on formica. Not only would it be heat-resistant, but it would be easy to wash.

QUAGMEYER: Well, I've never done anything quite like it before, but I suppose we all have to move with the times.

MRS. KRUMGOLD: Marvelous. Seymour, I told you.

MR. KRUMGOLD: Let's not start celebrating. We haven't talked price.

QUAGMEYER: I'm sure we can come to some agreement. But look here, there's one thing we've overlooked—the subject matter.

MRS. KRUMGOLD: Oh, who cares? So long as it doesn't clash with the drapes. They're silver blue.

MR. KRUMGOLD: And my mother comes to dinner every Friday night. It shouldn't be smutty.

MRS. KRUMGOLD: Well, now that it's all settled, when can we expect it?

QUAGMEYER: Never.

MRS. KRUMGOLD: I beg your pardon.

MR. KRUMGOLD: What kind of a way is this to do business?

QUACMEYER: My way.

MRS. KRUMGOLD (*Lightly*): Well—if that's how you feel about it. Could you recommend a good restaurant around here?

QUAGMEYER (*Inhales deeply*): Lady, I'm a quiet, middle-aged man with a receding hairline and most of my own teeth—by profession a painter.

MRS. KRUMGOLD: So?

QUAGMEYER: So every morning, while nine million people are rushing to Wall Street and the Garment Center and Radio City, I come here to my little nook and ply my craft. By no stretch of the imagination would you confuse me with Giotto or El Greco or Picasso, but I don't bother anyone.

MRS. KRUMGOLD: Look, there are plenty of other painters . . .

QUAGMEYER: Please—I'm not finished. Now, don't think I'm complaining. I make a mediocre living, but my career suits me. I'm adjusted to it, the way a maple tree manages to grow in a cement sidewalk. The only drawback to my existence, though, is the hyenas.

MRS. KRUMGOLD: The what?

QUAGMEYER: Every so often, the door opens and a couple of hyenas walk in. You can't tell they're hyenas because they walk like people, dress like people, and they have bank accounts—(GLORIA *rises indignantly*)—but you know 'em the minute they open their mouths. Well, I'll tell you how I protect myself. Over here behind the curtain, I keep a heavy club. First I warn them, and if they don't heed my warning, I count to ten and go for the club. (*Ominously*) One . . . two . . . three . . . four . . . (*The* KRUMGOLDS *exit precipitately*) five . . . six . . . seven, eight, nine, ten!

LANCE (*Openmouthed admiration*): That was an experience, Mr. Quagmeyer.

QUAGMEYER: Nothing unusual.

LANCE: Integrity in action. It was a privilege to see it.

QUAGMEYER (*Grimly*): Yes, no doubt.

LANCE: Mr. Quagmeyer, I'm just beginning to realize what discipline an artist has to have.

QUAGMEYER: Well, then, your time hasn't been wasted.

LANCE: If you had a secretary or an assistant, like, to protect you, you'd be free to concentrate.

QUAGMEYER: Are you proposing yourself for the post?

LANCE: I could be real helpful, Mr. Quagmeyer. I'll run errands, take messages, and in between, you could give me various pointers on your craft.

QUAGMEYER (*Nodding*): Like those apprentices the Old Masters used to have.

LANCE: That's it, sir—exactly!

QUAGMEYER: I see. Well, forget it. The last thing I need here is a *nudnick* asking a lot of damn fool questions.

LANCE: I wouldn't get in your way.

QUAGMEYER: I refuse to consider it, I tell you.

LANCE: Couldn't we give it a trial—please? If it didn't work out . . . (QUAGMEYER, *indomitable, shakes head*) Mr. Quagmeyer, when you were just beginning, didn't anyone ever lend you a hand?

QUAGMEYER (*A pause*): Well—O.K. (*As* LANCE *brightens*) But remember, you're on probation. If I bounce you into the street, no spaniel eyes or bawling—do you hear?

LANCE: Don't you worry.

QUAGMEYER: Right. (*Glances at wrist watch*) Now, look, the morning's shot. I've got to get some stretchers. While I'm gone, you can begin your first lesson.

LANCE: Yes, sir.

QUAGMEYER: In oil painting, the brushwork is everything (*Produces long-handled floor brush from behind stove*) Get into those corners. And if you shape up, I may let you wash the skylight.

> (HE *exits.* LANCE *stands holding brush, exhales slow sigh of delirious happiness. He moves about for a moment, inspecting studio. Then puts broom aside, timidly picks up palette and brush, poses himself in his conception of painter at work. A pause; then, heralded by a perfunctory knock at door,* HARRY HUBRIS, *a feisty, self-assured theatrical highbinder, enters bearing an attaché case*)

HUBRIS: Hi, there, Maestro. Harry Hubris—Hubbub Productions.

LANCE: Harry Hubris? The movie producer?

HUBRIS (*Surveys studio with distaste*): Say, are you kidding? Those terrific abstractions of yours—you don't actually *paint* them here?

LANCE: No, I'm only the apprentice. Mr. Quagmeyer's not here.

HUBRIS (*Amused scorn*): Listen, I know that dodge. Your dealer told me about your publicity phobia. (*Shakes head*) Go figure it. It always kills me an artist should hole up in a flea-bag to conceive a masterpiece. Still, everybody to their own ulcer.

LANCE: Mr. Hubris, I'm trying to tell you. I'm not Goddard Quagmeyer.

HUBRIS: Pops, will you drop dead on that Salinger kick? I recognized you the minute I walked in. And I want you to know that I consider you one of the nine foremost painters of our time.

LANCE: Who are the other eight?

HUBRIS: Don't get me started, pal. I've got maybe the most important collection in the L.A. area. Four Jackson Pollocks, three Ben Shahns, five Lipchitzes, one of yours—

LANCE: Which one?

HUBRIS (*Impatiently*): Ask my wife, that's her department. All I know is she bought it in 1956, right after I had my

thyroid out . . . But look here, let's get down to basics.
Did you perchance read *The Tortured Bostonian?*

LANCE: What is it?

HUBRIS: The biography of John Singer Sargent—by Irving
Stonehenge.

LANCE: Oh—oh, yes—I think I read the plot in *Time* Magazine. It was very intriguing.

HUBRIS: I'll tell you how intriguing. I paid two hundred and
seventy big ones for the picture rights. Just imagine Rob
Roy Fruitwell in the lead!

LANCE: Who is he?

HUBRIS: Rob Roy? Only the biggest potential draw in pictures today. Properly handled, Fruitwell could be another
Kirk Douglas, and—(*Lowers voice*)—I'll exhale you something in the strictest confidence. Next season you won't
be able to tell them apart—after Fruitwell has his dimple
deepened! But my immediate headache is this. Rob Roy's
a born actor, and he'll play the hell out of Sargent, but
what he requires is a little coaching from a professional
artist like you.

LANCE: How could anybody teach a man to paint in one
lesson?

HUBRIS: For God's sake, smarten up, will you? This lug
don't know from the muse. All you got to do is show him
how to hold a brush . . . (*Indicates palette*) what that
board is for . . . which end of the tube the paint comes
out. Two years ago he was a bus boy in Fort Wayne.

LANCE: I've never dealt with actors. I haven't any clue to their mentality.

HUBRIS: Mentality's one problem you won't have with Rob Roy Fruitwell. Strictly a matzo ball.

LANCE: But John Singer Sargent was a genius.

HUBRIS (*Triumphantly*): That's the beauty part. This cluck is a sensitized sponge that he'll soak up the info you give him and project it. So, in view of the fact that we start shooting Friday, I had Rob Roy sky in from the Coast last night solely on purpose to huddle with you.

LANCE (*Folding his arms*): Well, you're wasting your time, Mr. Hubris. There's one thing you'd better understand. Money won't buy everything.

HUBRIS: I consider that a highly un-American attitude. What are you, a Red or something?

LANCE: This is the studio of a dedicated painter—a person with ideals. You're asking a man to betray his birthright.

HUBRIS: You know, fellow, I'm disenchanted with you. You talk like a mouth-breather.

ROB ROY FRUITWELL (*From doorway*): Hey, Harry!

(HUBRIS's protégé slouches in, a standard prize bullock with Brando tonsure and capped teeth, in Sy Devore silks and gooseneck sweater exposing thorax. HUBRIS's irritation instantly turns to saccharine)

HUBRIS: Hiya, Rob Roy! What do you know, sweetheart?

ROB ROY (*Nose wrinkling as he looks around*): Man, where's the Board of Health? It's like Roachville here.

HUBRIS: Don't mind this rattrap, baby. In the picture, you're going to have a studio the size of Carnegie Hall.

ROB ROY: Big deal. O.K., come on—what's the action? I left a broad in the kip.

HUBRIS (*To* LANCE): It's a technical term. Rob Roy, this is the artist I told you about.

(ROB ROY *saunters toward easel, examines the picture on it intently*)

LANCE: But, Mr. Hubris—I'm trying to tell you—

ROB ROY: Hey, Jack, this doodle here. What's it supposed to be—a woman?

LANCE: Of course. Don't you see the female elements?

ROB ROY: Bud, you need therapy.

HUBRIS: Well, I wouldn't go that far, Rob Roy. You know, a artist reacts to the world around him cranium-wise—through the old noggin.

ROB ROY: Don't give me that bushwa. I've dated Mamie Van Doren, Jayne Mansfield and Diana Dors, and take it from me, Clyde, they don't have any corners. This moke's in trouble.

HUBRIS (*With wild gaiety*): Ha-ha—who isn't? Now, Rob Roy, doll, I just want to check on a couple of scenes to insure we don't pull a booboo. (*Whips open attaché case, produces smock and beret*) Here, slip these on so you'll get used to the feel.

ROB ROY: What the hell are we making, a costume picture? You said I wear a sweatshirt and jeans.

HUBRIS (*Dripping with sucrose*): In the love scenes, pussy-cat. But when you're like sketching and dreaming up your different masterpieces, we got to blueprint you're a artist. It establishes your identity.

ROB ROY: The way a sheriff puts on a tin star?

HUBRIS: Or a bus boy his white coat.

ROB ROY (*Reacts, wheels toward* HUBRIS): What did you say?

HUBRIS: Me? Not a thing, honey—nothing. (*Muttering,* ROB ROY *dons smock in reverse.* HUBRIS *gropes a script from attaché case*) Now, first of all, Rob Roy, run through the situation where Vincent Youmans tries to win you back to your wife.

LANCE: Vincent Youmans, the composer? How does he come into this?

HUBRIS: A dramatic license we took to justify the score. You see, Youmans is a young music student at Harvard that Sargent befriends. Can you remember the lines, Rob Roy?

ROB ROY (*Contorting forehead*): I don't know. There's a coupla hard words.

HUBRIS: Never mind. Spitball some dialogue to give the sense. Go ahead, I'll cue you. I'll be Youmans. (*Declamatory*) "Good morrow, Sargent!"

ROB ROY (*Tonelessly*): Hello, Youmans. Where you been, man?

HUBRIS (*Round-eyed with admiration*): And he don't even know Lee Strasberg! (*Reads dialogue from script*) "Oh, just studying my counterpoint over in Cambridge. But you certainly are a storm center these days, John Singer. All Beacon Hill is agog the way you threw up your job as stockbroker and abandoned your family. Can a pair of saucy blue eyes underlie this move, as waggling tongues imply?"

ROB ROY (*With a purportedly cynical hoot*): Women! I'm tired of those silly little creatures casting their spell on me. I want to paint—to *paint*, do you hear? (*Hoarsely*) I've got to express what I feel deep down inside me! The agony, the heartbreak!

HUBRIS: Beautiful—beautiful! Sweetheart, don't change a word, a syllable! Do that on camera, and I'll guarantee you an Oscar! (*Wheeling toward* LANCE) How did it sound? Does it ring true from the artist's point of view?

LANCE: Well, yes, on the whole, but I noticed one thing wrong. Mr. Fruitwell's got his smock on backwards.

HUBRIS: You're dead right—the audience might mistake him for a barber. Watch that, Rob Roy.

ROB ROY (*As one crucified*): Damn it, Harry, you gonna hang around this mother-grabbin' place all night? I got an eight-man team of writers from the New York *Post* waiting to interview me!

HUBRIS: Be patient another ten seconds, kid, I got to corroborate one more detail. The key scene where you get your big break from the hotel manager. The plot point here, Maestro, is that Sargent's down and out in New York. It's Christmas Day, the landlord's shut off the gas, and he's starving.

LANCE: The landlord is?

HUBRIS: No, no—Sargent. (*Sorely impatient*) Anyway, just at his darkest hour, in comes Tuesday Weld, the hat check girl at the St. Regis Hotel, which she's been secretly in love with him. She's persuaded the hotel manager to let Sargent paint a mural of Old King Cole . . . in the men's room. (LANCE *nods*) How would a painter react in those circumstances? What exact phraseology would he employ?

LANCE (*Ponders*): Well, let me see . . . Sometimes they smite their forehead—(*Demonstrates*)—and use a simple Greek word, like "Eureka!"

ROB ROY (*Ripping off smock*): And for this you fly me from the Coast, you *schlep!*

HUBRIS: I only did it for your good, baby!

ROB ROY (*Raging*): Don't try to con me, you muzzler! I'm walking off your stinking picture!

HUBRIS: Now calm down, you're tired—

ROB ROY: You bet I am! Tired of being pushed around by you and that turpentine peddler! I'm calling my agent, Monroe Sweetmeat, right now to break my contract!

HUBRIS (*Panicky*): Rob Roy, I sensed you were unhappy in this role—I had a premonition. I've decided to buy you the property you begged me for—*Laughing Stevedore*. Tomorrow I ink a new pact with Monroe that doubles your salary to five-fifty a week!

ROB ROY: Ink your head off! You're a loser, Hubris. I'm planing to Rome tonight to see Carlo Ponti!

HUBRIS (*Agonized*): Ponti?

ROB ROY: You heard me!

HUBRIS: That pizza peddler! What can he give you?

ROB ROY: Top billing and some of the greatest zook in Europe!

HUBRIS: Yeah? (*Scrabbles in pockets, extracts a fragment of paper, and thrusting it at him, speaks sotto voce*) Can Carlo Ponti give you that? Answer me!

ROB ROY: "April Monkhood, 33 Perry Street." (*His eyes narrow lustfully*) Is she built? Is she stacked?

HUBRIS: Who cares? She's alive and she's there!

ROB ROY (*Starting toward door*): Come on!

HUBRIS: Go ahead—I'll folly you ... (*Turning back to* LANCE, *with intense conviction*) A household word in two years! That's what I predict for that young man!

LANCE (*Dubiously*): Yes, he seems to be very gifted—

HUBRIS: He's a lot more than that, Buster. He's going to be an annuity for my old age. Well, thanks for the dope you gave me. (*His voice sweetens*) Say, Rembrandt—in view of all the publicity you're getting, you ought to present me with a little token of your esteem. This sketch here, for instance . . .

(*As* HE *starts to remove painting from easel,* QUAG-MEYER *enters carrying a couple of stretchers*)

QUAGMEYER: What are you doing there? Leave that alone!

HUBRIS (*Belligerently*): Yeah? Why should I?

QUAGMEYER: Because it's mine, that's why. Drop it, I said!

HUBRIS (*Puzzled, to* LANCE): Who is this bird?

LANCE: He's Mr. Quagmeyer—the one you came here to see! (*To* QUAGMEYER) I tried to tell him I wasn't you, but he was too bullheaded to listen!

HUBRIS (*Easily*): Oh well, what's the diff, so long as we finally connected? Quagmeyer, I'm Harry Hubris of Hubbub Productions in Hollywood. I badly need a technical adviser for my new picture based on the life of John Singer Sargent.

QUAGMEYER (*Turning away*): Save your breath, Mr. Hubris. You just want to use my name to merchandise your junk.

HUBRIS: Yeah? Well, you listen to me, pal! What if I gave you complete control over the whole artistic end?

QUAGMEYER: You mean absolute authority?

HUBRIS (*Transported*): I'll tell you how absolute. You need a certain statue from the Louvre? I'll glom it for you. You want a particular type beret for Sargent's head? I'll steam it for you. You'll be the chief shamus of the whole goddam production!

QUAGMEYER: Well, that's different.

HUBRIS: You bet your rosy pratt it is. Now, as to the fee, we don't expect anything free gratis. I'm buying a reputation, and I'm prepared to lay it on the line.

QUAGMEYER: What did you have in mind?

HUBRIS: One-fifty a week, a four-week guarantee, and your transportation.

QUAGMEYER: That doesn't seem like very much ...

HUBRIS: Fifteen hundred a week!

QUAGMEYER: We're in business.

LANCE (*Outraged*): Mr. Quagmeyer, how can you lend yourself to such practices? I thought you had some integrity— that you stood for something clean and straight and fine. But there's nothing people won't do for the almighty dollar, is there? ... O.K., go ahead and sell your soul to the Devil. I for one won't watch it!

(HE *storms out*)

HUBRIS (*Blandly*): Typical. A rebel without a cause. (HE *dismisses it with a wave*) But getting back to our deal, Quag. Instead of fifteen hundred in a lump sum, what about thirty-five dollars down, fifty at the preview, and the balance the minute the negative cost is paid off? (*Energetically*) Or maybe you'd prefer ten bucks now and a percentage deal, like a half share of the Transylvanian rights? As a matter of fact, you stand to make twice as much dough that way . . .

(*As* HE *closes in on* QUAGMEYER, *fraternally clasping his shoulders, we segue into—*)

Act I

SCENE 5

SCENE: APRIL MONKHOOD'S apartment.

TIME: The same.

AT RISE: APRIL'S housewarming—specifically, its cocktail phase—is in progress. MAURICE BLOUNT, a fly-by-night publisher, BORIS PICKWICK, a flautist, CHENILLE SCHREI-BER, a beatnik, and several other unemployables grouped downstage chattering ad lib. APRIL hurries in from kitchen bearing tray of drinks. Subdued Muzak audible in background. The KRUMGOLDS enter, look about fascinated.

APRIL (Distractedly): Now who hasn't met who? Oh, Gloria! Maurice, do you know the Krumgolds? They're earth people. Gloria! Seymour! (To latter) Maurice Blount's one of our most distinguished publishers of erotica . . .

MR. KRUMGOLD: I'm in the textile-shrinking game.

MRS. KRUMGOLD: A publisher . . . how fascinating!

APRIL: And Seymour, this is Boris Pickwick, first flautist of the Utica Symphony . . . Chenille Schreiber . . .

PICKWICK: Where's Vernon?

APRIL: Oh, he'll be along in a wink. (*to* KRUMGOLD) Vernon Equinox, that is. He writes non-prose for magazines like *Angst* and he also paints under the influence of mescaline.

MR. KRUMGOLD: I once smoked a reefer with a couple of girls from Bayonne, and boy, was I sick.

MRS. KRUMGOLD: Nobody wants to hear about your orgies.

> (THEY *exchange glances of hatred, separate.* KITTY ENTRAIL, *an intense minor poetess in paisley and hoop earrings, enters with* VERNON EQUINOX)

APRIL: Kitty, how divine to see you! But where's Rolf?

KITTY: He couldn't come, he's laid up with an impacted hip.

APRIL: I'll send him two pounds of caviar tomorrow.

VERNON: Who are all these people? My dear, it's the copulation explosion!

APRIL (*Pouncing on him*): Vernon, when did you get back from Haiti?

VERNON: Oaxaca. Nobody goes to Haiti any more.

APRIL: Of course—I forgot.

VERNON: Not Oaxaca proper, mind you. A tiny village sixty miles south—San Juan Doloroso. Sabu and I lived there for three pesos a day.

APRIL: Incredible. But I suppose it's already spoiled.

VERNON: Not inside the volcano. Only on the rim.

KITTY: Darling, I adore your new *ambiente*. It's too Aubrey Beardsley, isn't it, Vernon?

VERNON (*Critically*): Hm-m-m, I'm not sure about that area over there. I'd like to see a Renaissance credenza.

KITTY: Or rather, the memory of a credenza.

APRIL (*To* MR. KRUMGOLD):This is Kitty Entrail, the poetess ... Seymour Krumgold.

KITTY: *Enchanté*.

MR. KRUMGOLD: I'm in the textile-shrinking game.

APRIL: Kitty is a minor poetess.

MR. KRUMGOLD: A poetess, eh? I always wanted to know— what do you get for a poem?

KITTY: Heartbreak, Mr. Krumgold, heartbreak.

MR. KRUMGOLD: Same in the textile game.

BLOUNT (*To* MRS. KRUMGOLD): I can't believe it! Did I un- derstand you never read the memoirs of Polly Adler? You missed one of the great experiences!

MRS. KRUMGOLD: What is it, some kind of a historical work?

BLOUNT: No, more of a true-confessions type thing. I'll mail you a copy tomorrow in a plain wrapper.

MRS. KRUMGOLD (*Archly*): Do I have to read it in a plain wrapper?

BLOUNT: I got a closetful of fancy ones. Come up to my place and we'll read it together.

MRS. KRUMGOLD (*Slaps his hand away*): Don't get fresh with me, you measle.

BLOUNT (*With dignity, exiting*): Excuse me, I got to correct some proofs.

CHENILLE (*Impassioned, to* PICKWICK): But, Boris, Mac-Dougal Alley's the very reason I left Bridgeport.

PICKWICK: The trouble with MacDougal Alley is, it has only two dimensions. The people over there is strictly a lot of cheap crumbs. Now in my winter home, in Cortina d'Ampezzo—

KITTY: Cortina d'Ampezzo! The echolalia of that name! It's so—so steeped in the bright black creosote of authenticity.

PICKWICK: You see what I mean?

KITTY (*Ecstatically*): Oh, I do, I do!

PICKWICK: Then explain it to me.

KITTY (*Recoiling from* CHENILLE): Get that woman away from me!

APRIL: Vernon, I'm furious with you. Everyone's avid to see those puppets you twist out of pipe cleaners.

VERNON: I'm through with that dilettante stuff. I've been designing some nonobjective marionettes—a combination of dance and mime. Aaron Copland's wild to do the music.

APRIL: Oh, do let him!

MR. KRUMGOLD (*To* MRS. KRUMGOLD): Ah, shut up!

APRIL: How do you like the Krumgolds, by the way?

VERNON (*Sincerely—eating canapé*): They're the most delicious things I've ever eaten.

(LANCE *enters, spots* APRIL *in the crush, calls to her*)

LANCE: April! April!

APRIL: Lance Weatherwax! Whatever in the world are you doing here?

LANCE: You invited me.

APRIL: Then where have you been, for God's sake? I've had to do everything myself!

LANCE: I'm sorry, April, I had a terrible experience. I went over to see Goddard Quagmeyer about my problem.

APRIL: You can tell me all about it tomorrow. Run and get a muscatel for Kitty.

LANCE: I will, but when you hear what that man did—

APRIL (*Impatiently*): Now, really, Lance, is this the time or place to air your petty personal concerns? (*Turning toward* guests—*raises voice*) Out in the hall, everybody! Dinner's ready on the stairs!

(*As the guests, chattering animatedly, drift off,* LANCE *delays* APRIL)

LANCE: You told me to go see him—

APRIL: Who?

LANCE: Quagmeyer. You were wrong—he's as corrupt as anybody else.

APRIL: Are you still harping on him?

LANCE: Anybody that sells out his principles for fifteen hundred dollars. It was disgusting! You wouldn't believe it. There was this movie actor there—Rob Roy Fruitwell—

APRIL: Rob Roy Fruitwell! That hoodlum! I've seen those movies of his. He's an animal!

LANCE: I'll admit he's very masculine, but Mr. Quagmeyer—

APRIL: Masculine? He's like something out of the primordial ooze. Is that what you admire in people?

LANCE: No—no—no—

APRIL: Lance, I'm surprised at you, I detest everything he stands for.

LANCE: Yes, yes—but Mr. Quagmeyer . . .

APRIL: I know his type, believe me. He thinks all he has to do is look at a girl, nod in her direction—(ROB ROY *enters, strolls past* APRIL *with a meaningful glance, and starts to exit*)—and she'll go lusting after him.

(APRIL *follows* ROB ROY *out*)

LANCE: April!

(HARRY HUBRIS *appears jovially from the outer world*)

HUBRIS: Say, have you seen Rob Roy Fruitwell?

LANCE: She's gone!

HUBRIS (*Recognizing* LANCE): Why, it's the mouth-breather. (*Chuckles*) I got to hand it to you, Clyde, I really mistook you for a painter before.

LANCE (*Brokenly*): I knew it couldn't last. I was only deceiving myself.

HUBRIS: Well, you fooled me, and I'm a pretty tough customer.

LANCE: She's left me—abandoned me. Oh, what am I going to do?

HUBRIS: For openers you could clean up these olive pits.

LANCE: She was my guiding star—my beacon . . . But there's no point in life any more.

HUBRIS: Hey, Willie, you need some fresh air. (*Looks at initial on* LANCE'S *sweater*) Back to the "Y" and take a cold shower.

LANCE (*Bitterly*): I've been on the wrong track all along. What good is art if it just leads to heartbreak?

HUBRIS: Say, this is a soul in torment.

LANCE: I'm through with the ivory tower. I'm going to work in the mass media. I'll show her what beauty I can create!

HUBRIS (*Patronizingly*): Listen, bub, what are you—a chicken-flicker? An elevator operator in a one-story building?

LANCE: One day when I'm immortal, she'll know the sacrifices I made.

HUBRIS: Sacrifices? A rabbi—is that what you are?

LANCE: She'll remember me to her dying day, you wait. She'll remember the name of Lance Weatherwax.

HUBRIS: (*Electrified*): Lance Weatherwax? My God, not the Weatherwax All-Weather Garbage Disposal Plan?

LANCE: Yes.

HUBRIS: Then I'll tell you what you are, kid—you're a movie director! (*Smiting him mightily*) You're going to direct my new picture, *The Guns of Appomatox!* The biggest grosser in the next ten years! The Music Hall's got it penciled in for Easter Week, and it's not even written yet! And you're the bozo that's going to direct it!

LANCE: I never directed before—

HUBRIS: A fresh mind, a primitive! Willie Wyler wants to do it but he's too shallow. John Huston wants it—he's too deep. You're the logical man!

LANCE: Golly, sir, are you really serious?

HUBRIS (*Encircling* LANCE's *shoulders*): I'll tell you how serious. To show my faith in you, I'm going to let your folks put up the money for an independent production! (*As* HE *steers* LANCE *out*) Hollywood—here you come!

CURTAIN

ct Two

Act II

SCENE 1

SCENE: *The Rising Sun Domestic Employment Agency, a modest establishment in Santa Barbara, California. The furnishings are simple: a desk, matching chair and filing cabinet, wall calendar, a large photo of the Del Monte coastline with twisted cypresses.*

TIME: *Morning, two weeks later.*

AT RISE: MRS. YOUNGHUSBAND, *a desiccated gentlewoman in her forties, professionally hochgeboren and attired in a cardigan sweater set and pearls, sits at desk, speaks animatedly into phone.*

MRS. YOUNGHUSBAND: Now, Chang Fat, I have a simply marvelous situation for you—a yachtsman down at Balboa. He's got a sixty-three-foot yawl with a balloon jib, and he needs a wideawake Chinese boy to do for him . . . What? . . . No—only the summer. In the winter, he lives at Pancreas Hall, that sanitarium in Glendale. No, poor man, he thinks a weevil is eating his liver. All right, then, three o'clock. Goodbye.

HUBRIS (*Entering, arms outstretched*): Dolores, Dolores, Dolores!

MRS. YOUNGHUSBAND (*Toothily*): So generous of you to come up to Santa Barbara, Mr. Hubris. I know how valuable your time is.

HUBRIS: Dolores, Tom Younghusband—your husband, may he rest in peace—was the greatest stunt man that ever worked for me. The day that Egyptian temple fell on him, I made a resolve his widow would never want for a thing.

MRS. YOUNGHUSBAND: There should be more people like you, Mr. Hubris. This world would be a better place.

HUBRIS: Of course . . . Now, you said you got a problem. You said you got a client needs a first-rate houseboy.

MRS. YOUNGHUSBAND: The Rising Sun Domestic Employment Agency handles only top-quality Oriental personnel.

HUBRIS: I got him, I got him—a Cambodian.

MRS. YOUNGHUSBAND: These people, Mr. and Mrs. Fingerhead, are terribly particular. One thing they won't tolerate is a jazz baby. You know the type gook I mean.

HUBRIS: They can rest easy, dear lady. Wing Loo studied three years at U.C.L.A. He was on the dean's list morning, noon and night.

MRS. YOUNGHUSBAND: And you can vouch for his cooking, can you?

HUBRIS: Don't ask *me!* Ask a gourmet like Darryl Zanuck —Hedda Hopper—Duke Wayne—people which they make a shrine of their stomach. Every time I throw a *luau,* they're in the kitchen trying to hire Wing Loo away from me.

MRS. YOUNGHUSBAND: An authentic Cambodian, you said?

HUBRIS (*Rising*): Right off the boat—a greenhorn. You'll see for yourself. (*Calls through door*) Wing Loo, Wing Loo! LANCE *enters, his appearance perceptibly altered. He wears Chinese garb, his eyes have a strikingly Oriental slant, and his skin is a distinct yellow. Carries a cheap cardboard suitcase*) Did I exaggerate?

MRS. YOUNGHUSBAND: Yes, he's the real thing, all right.

HUBRIS: Like night and day from a false Cambodian.

MRS. YOUNGHUSBAND: You've just had the most glowing reference, Wing Loo. I hope you create a good impression on the Fingerheads, now.

LANCE: It sounds like a golden opportunity.

MRS. YOUNGHUSBAND: It is.

HUBRIS (*Elaborate nonchalance*): Ah—correct me if I'm wrong, but you said the lady of the house is a writer, no?

MRS. YOUNGHUSBAND: Her husband, too. They're both experts on the Civil War. Written scads of books about it . . . Well, it's all set. If you'll excuse me, I have to run next door to the vegetarian bar. I have a very serious iron deficiency. The doctors gave me only nine hours to live. I have to go get my parsnip juice.

HUBRIS (*As* SHE *exits*): A parsnip condition, she should wear a metal tag. (*Energetically*) Now, look—we can't waste any time. You remember my instructions?

LANCE: To find out the plot of Mrs. Fingerhead's new Civil War novel. The one I'm going to direct.

HUBRIS: Right.

LANCE: Golly, Mr. Hubris, it was a great day when I met you. And now I'm going to express myself in film. Directing movies—(*Gratefully*) You sure have been swell, Mr. Hubris.

HUBRIS: Nothing at all—nothing at all.

LANCE: The only thing . . . (*Indicates make-up*) What does all this have to do with making movies?

HUBRIS: It's the most important part—stealing the property! Everybody in the trade'll be shooting a Civil War spectacular on account of it's the Centennial. We got to be there fustest with the mostest—*vershsteh?*

LANCE (*Dubiously*): I guess so . . .

HUBRIS: You're the undercover man, the camera eye recording every little detail. And if you can heist the manuscript, so much the better.

LANCE: The whole thing?

HUBRIS: As much as you can carry. How's the make-up?

LANCE: The adhesive tape hurts my eyes.

HUBRIS: Take it off at night. But don't forget—keep that Jap-a-lac on your face, and lots of Scuff-Coat on the hair.

LANCE: What about the meals?

HUBRIS: Don't worry. They're Southerners. Just look mysterious and give 'em grits.

LANCE: Suppose they order something fancy.

HUBRIS: I'll send you a couple of books. *The Joy of Cooking,* and *Love and Knishes* by Sara Kasdan.

LANCE: Mr. Hubris—what I'm doing—are you sure it's legal? Couldn't I get arrested?

HUBRIS: For what? Impersonating a Cambodian?

LANCE: It just doesn't seem right.

HUBRIS: Of course it ain't! It's sneaky—low-down—beneath contempt! But you listen to me. Suppose Harry Lime refused to water down that black-market penicillin in *The Third Man.* Suppose Janet Leigh didn't take that shower in *Psycho.* Suppose Simone Signoret didn't shack up with that goy in *Room at the Top?* Where would this great industry be today?

LANCE: Gosh, I never thought of it that way.

HUBRIS: Of course!

(As THEY exit, HUBRIS *registering satisfaction at the logic that has convinced* LANCE, *we segue to—)*

Act II

SCENE 2

SCENE: Kitchen of the FINGERHEAD residence. Windows rear over a sink unit flanked by work counters and cupboards. Wall phone. At center stage, a table bearing a silver pitcher, creamer, spoons and forks, candlesticks, silver polish, rags.

TIME: Noon, five days later.

AT RISE: LANCE, in houseman's striped apron, is polishing silver. Muted music from transistor on table before him. After a moment, GRACE FINGERHEAD enters from living room wearing a floppy garden hat, carries flower basket containing shears over arm.

GRACE: Good morning, Wing Loo!

LANCE: Good morning, Mrs. Fingerhead.

GRACE: The lobelias look so lovely this morning I can't resist them. I'm going down to the lower garden and snip off their little pods.

LANCE: Yes, ma'am.

GRACE: Whose motorcycle was that I heard in the driveway just now?

LANCE: The fish market with our order.

GRACE: Oh, your halibut squares . . . Wing Loo, I know you're making every effort, but I wish you'd stick to the menu I give you. Now that noodle ring you made yesterday—

LANCE: I'm sorry, Mrs. Fingerhead. I guess I put in too many raisins.

GRACE: And just because your last employer loved frozen blintzes, I see no reason to get them three nights running.

LANCE: Yes, ma'am.

GRACE: Is Mr. Fingerhead up yet?

LANCE: No, ma'am. He worked all night again. I heard him dictating into his machine.

GRACE: A lot of good it'll do him. My book'll be out long before his. Congratulate me. Wing Loo, I've just completed the final chapter—the burning of Natchez.

LANCE (Reacting): Oh? You're all finished?

GRACE: Four years' work. Why, I've *discarded* more than a million and a half words. Even so, the manuscript runs to eleven hundred pages.

LANCE: I hope Madam will have a great success.

GRACE: Thank you, dear, I feel I deserve it. Nobody before ever looked at the Confederacy through the eyes of a Creole call girl. Call me visionary, Wing Loo, but some day the character of Stephanie Lavabeau will stand with

Madame Bovary and Becky Sharp. (*Picks up clipping from desk*) What's this?

LANCE: The boss left it here for you. He cut it out of the *New York Times* Book Review.

GRACE (*Hands it to him*): What does it say?

LANCE: "Curtis Fingerhead, one of our most constant observers of the Southern literary scene—"

GRACE (*Angrily*): What are they talking about, the idiots? I've observed it twice as much as he has!

LANCE: "—is promising a new novel for the fall season based on the loves of Stonewall Jackson."

GRACE (*Snatches clipping, crumples it*): Promising is right! He wrote two chapters of the wretched thing and bogged down. And even if he got it done, I doubt whether he'd sell twelve copies.

(CURTIS FINGERHEAD *enters, attired in bathrobe*)

CURTIS: I heard that! And may I observe that anyone whose conception of the Union breastworks at Vicksburg is so Freudian—

GRACE: Thank you, my dear. I didn't realize you'd ever read my best seller, *Spoon Bread and Powderhorns.*

CURTIS: I haven't, but I occasionally do run across your reviews. (*Producing clipping from bathrobe pocket*) This one, for instance, from the Nashville *Scimitar*: "Author Grace Fingerhead betrays her usual ineptitude—"

GRACE: Mr. Fingerhead! Must you vent your spleen in front of the help? Not that I think Wing Loo is indiscreet.

CURTIS: Oh, I've met a couple of gabby Chinks in my time. Boy, did they run off at the mouth! (*Chuckles*) Or maybe it was two other Chinamen, they all look alike to me.

GRACE: I doubt whether Wing Loo is interested in your past.

CURTIS: I'm interested in his. Bet you saw plenty of orgies down there in Hollywood, eh? (LANCE *lowers eyes modestly*) Lots of naked starlets chasing around in—what do they call 'em—teddies?

GRACE: Curtis, what a thing to say.

CURTIS: Ah, everybody knows what goes on. Swimming pools full of champagne, mixed bathing—

GRACE: Well, Wing Loo won't encounter that type of thing at our house.

CURTIS: No, he sure won't.

(HE *exits*)

GRACE (*To* LANCE, *her voice quivering*): Do you want to know how downright evil some people can be? I've a notion he's trying to steal the manuscript of my book!

LANCE (*Petrified*): Ma'am?

GRACE: Well, you've noticed that old-fashioned safe upstairs in my closet—behind my dresses?

LANCE: Uh—I'm not sure . . .

GRACE: Oh, naturally, you'd have no reason to be poking around up there, but anyway, that's where I keep it, the manuscript, that is, and someone's been fooling with the combination recently. I put some axle grease on the knob a day or two ago, and sure enough, it's all smudged!

LANCE: Why—why would Mr. Fingerhead do a thing like that?

GRACE: Because he's consumed with jealousy, don't you see? It's killing him that Emmett Stagg, the head of Charnel House, wants to publish it. (*Sharp bark of laughter*) Well, Curtis won't get away with it. I bought a fingerprint kit!

LANCE: Holy Moses.

GRACE (*Shrugs*): Oh, well, perhaps one should be more compassionate. His last urinalysis came out 94 per cent cognac.

(SHE *exits*. LANCE *crosses swiftly to phone, dials*)

LANCE: Hello? Is this Hubbub Productions? Extension 354— Yes, yes, it's urgent! Listen, Miriam, this is Lance again— I have to speak to Mr. Hubris right away . . . Where is he, then? You *have* to find him—get a message to him . . . He *knows* that. I told him all about Stephanie Lavabeau —I told him it was in the safe but I couldn't—what? Look—tell him I'm in danger, they suspect something—

GRACE (*Offstage*): Wing Loo!

LANCE: I got to hang up, someone's coming—

GRACE (*Excitedly re-enters*): Wing Loo—Wing Loo! I have the most thrilling surprise for you! Guess who just walked into the laundry area! Your father! From Cambodia!

(As LANCE *emits a startled exclamation,* HARRY HUBRIS *enters past her.* HE *too is garbed as a Chinese, implemented by a Manchu-style pigtail, and carries an old-fashioned portmanteau*)

HUBRIS (*Emotionally, as he beholds* LANCE): My little tiger-cub. Come to me, pride of your ancestors.

(LANCE, *frozen with fright, advances to him, bobs jerkily*)

LANCE: Honored sire.

(THEY *kowtow elaborately to each other.* HUBRIS, *tiring abruptly of the charade, brings* LANCE *up short*)

HUBRIS: Enough already!

GRACE (*With intense awe*): Filial respect . . . it's a tradition . . .

HUBRIS (*Turns to her, speaks in stilted English*): Five thousand years ago, the sage Matzo Tongue hath said, "If a pepper seed take wing, it will turn into a dragonfly. Yet if a dragonfly loses its wing, it will not turn into a pepper seed." That is what the sage hath said, five thousand years ago.

GRACE: The inscrutable wisdom of the East. (*Sighs*) But I mustn't intrude—you two have so much to say to each other.

(SHE *nods graciously to* HUBRIS, *exits*)

HUBRIS: O.K., enough with the laundryman bit. Where's the safe?

LANCE: Mr. Hubris, I just called you—we're in trouble!

HUBRIS: (*Reassuringly, indicates portmanteau*): Relax. The tools I got there can open anything.

GRACE (*Offstage*): Wing Loo-oo!

> (LANCE *hastily lapses into Chinese as* GRACE *reappears*)

HUBRIS: Vuss?

GRACE: Wing Loo, do offer your father a cup of oolong. He looks exhausted.

> (SHE *exits*)

LANCE: The safe's upstairs.

HUBRIS: Well, go and get it!

LANCE (*Horrified*): You mean, carry the whole safe out?

HUBRIS: Certainly. You're a big strong boy, you could lift a house. I can't lift on account of my thyroid, but I'll supervise. (*Energetically*) Here's the action. First—you're positive the whole script is inside, no loose fragments laying around?

LANCE: No, it's all there. She told me the plot—it's mostly sex.

HUBRIS: That's the two most important drives: Sex and what I got—hunger. O.K., you beat it upstairs and carry the box down while I stand guard. *Capisco?*

LANCE: But we're going to need a truck, or a car—

HUBRIS: I made a deal with a motorcycle kid from a fish market. The safe goes into the sidecar, and the two of us can hang onto the kid. Go on, now, upstairs and work fast.

(LANCE *picks up portmanteau and exits.* HUBRIS *runs to swinging door, hears someone coming and hides behind the counter.* CURTIS *enters swinging door, goes stealthily across stage and out.* FISH-MARKET BOY *enters, looks around, goes out swinging door.* GRACE *enters, looks around, sees* HUBRIS, *screams, and exits through swinging door.* EMMETT STAGG—*owl-faced, bouncy, bespectacled, a pipe stuck jauntily in teeth —enters.* HE *surveys kitchen cursorily, exits.* HUBRIS *reappears from behind counter, crosses to swinging door, listens, and then runs to table.* HE *scoops up silverware and starts to stuff it into his coat.* GRACE *enters swinging door humming to herself.* HUBRIS *drops silver and stands immobile*)

GRACE (*Aside, to audience*): So my envious husband plots to steal my manuscript, does he? Well, I'll fix his wagon. Here it is, transferred to microfilm, and all that remains is to smuggle it out of the house. Hello—this guileless Oriental is meet for my purpose. (*To* HUBRIS) Well, Mr. Loo, how did you find your son?

HUBRIS: I rook around—I see him.

GRACE: Ha-ha—very nicely phrased. By the way, Mr. Loo, would you do me a favor when you leave here?

HUBRIS: Me do anysing fo' plitty lady.

GRACE: Would you just drop this in the nearest mailbox? It's a wedding present for my niece.

HUBRIS (*Placing package in pocket*): Me keepum light here, missy, next to ticker.

GRACE: Why, how gallant of you, Mr. Loo. I'm much obriged.

HUBRIS: *Obliged.*

GRACE: Of course. Thank you so much.

HUBRIS (*Bowing her off*): My preasure. My preasure.

GRACE: Charming. You're too kind.

> (SHE *exits.* HUBRIS *assures himself* SHE *is safely out of the way, recrosses to living-room door and looks off anxiously.* HE *then returns to table at center, narrowly inspects silver service as though contemplating possibility of lifting it.* CURTIS *enters furtively, steals downstage.* HUBRIS *pretends to polish silver energetically*)

CURTIS (*Aside*): Well, my devious stratagems are coming to fruition at last. (*Exhibits duplicate of* GRACE's *package*) Thanks to technological advance, I now possess a duplicate microfilm copy of Grace's novel. To fob it off as my own, I shall need a cat's-paw. (*Descries* HUBRIS *upstage*) By Jove, the very man. This wily Oriental, skilled in intrigue, is meet for my purpose . . . I say there, Wing Loo!

HUBRIS: Yassuh, Bwana?

CURTIS (*Stares at him*): Humph. I don't know what it is about Santa Barbara, but it sure ages people. Boy, can you run an errand for me chop chop?

HUBRIS: Solly, no can do. Missy tell me stay here, shine silber.

CURTIS: Banana oil! I'm the one that pays your salary, do you hear? (HUBRIS *bobs assent*—CURTIS *starts writing address on package*) Now, run down and mail this manuscript for me.

HUBRIS (*Pricking up ears*): Manusclipt?

CURTIS: Yes, you wouldn't understand, but it's my novel of the Confederacy as seen through the eyes of a Creole call girl.

HUBRIS (*Reaches eagerly for it*): Yes, siree. Me complihend!

(*Takes package*)

CURTIS (*Regains package, rises*): On second thought, maybe I shouldn't entrust it to the mails.

HUBRIS: Me velly careful—me insure it!

(*Recaptures package*)

CURTIS: No, wait a minute (HE *forcibly takes package*) Film's got to be packed in a fireproof container—

HUBRIS (*Attempting to wrest package away*): Me pack it!

CURTIS (*Suspiciously, thrusting it behind him*): Oh, no, you won't, you cunning heathen. Nobody's handling this but yours truly—(*He throws off* HUBRIS *by main force*)—not after the pains it's cost me!

(CURTIS *exits, leaving* HUBRIS *fuming. An instant later,* STAGG *re-enters from living room*)

STAGG: Grace! Grace! Anybody home? (*Breezily*) Hi, there, John. I'm Emmett Stagg, Mrs. Fingerhead's publisher. I'm on my semiannual lecture tour of the West Coast, playing to packed houses everywhere, and thought I'd stop in.

HUBRIS: I bereave I see you on terevision.

STAGG: Every Sunday night unless you're blind. (*Impatiently*) Well, I can't wait, Lenny Bruce and eighteen of America's foremost sick comics are throwing me a—ha-ha —Stagg dinner at Hillcrest. (*Fumbles out calling card and pencil*) Here's my number—I'm staying with Tony Curtis in Bel Air.

HUBRIS: Tory Curis.

STAGG: You're dead right, Tony wouldn't want his phone bruited about. Tell you what, I'll leave Burt Lancaster's . . .

(*Writes behind table. As* HE *bends down to write,* CURTIS *re-enters*)

CURTIS: Where's that almond-eyed son-of-a-bitch was in here a minute ago?

STAGG: Hello—ha-ha—Fingerhead—

CURTIS: Emmett! What are you doing in this neck of the woods?

STAGG: I'm on my semiannual lecture tour of the West Coast—playing to packed houses everywhere—thought I'd drop in.

CURTIS: Fine. But why am I being so cordial to you? You're only here to see Grace.

STAGG: Curtis, that was unfair. Bring me a piece of work you've got faith in, and by tarnation, I'll paint your name across the sky!

CURTIS: You think that pipsqueak firm of yours is big enough to handle a runaway best seller?

STAGG: Who copped the National Book Award last year? Charnel House—with our number-one smash hit, *A Child's Life of Liberace.*

CURTIS (*Querulously*): I've got a taste in my mouth like a motorman's shoe. Where's that slippery Mongolian? (HE *catches sight of* HUBRIS) Hey, you! Fix me a highball—and heavy on the brandy.

HUBRIS: Velly good. I bling bottle.

(HE *exits*)

STAGG: Curtis, I see a sly little look in your eye. (*Wheedling*) Have you got a book in the oven?

CURTIS: A book, for God's sake? A cataclysm—a Vesuvius!

STAGG: You think there's a movie in it?

CURTIS: Ho-ho—and how! Why, there are scenes in it that'll make Grace Metalious look like Mother Goose! (HUBRIS *re-enters with brandy*) Wait till you read about the orgies at Rebel headquarters, the mixed bathing! No one before has ever looked at the Confederacy through the eyes of a Creole call girl.

STAGG: Man, we'll have to print that on asbestos—

CURTIS: All honeysuckle and spitfire—that's Stephanie Lava-beau!

(HUBRIS *reacts*)

STAGG: Who?

HUBRIS: Stephanie Lavabeau . . .

CURTIS (*Gleefully*): See that, Emmett? That heathen ignites at the name, and he doesn't even speak the language.

STAGG (*Excitedly*): Now, listen to me, pal, because I mean business. You let me have that book and I'll print a hundred and fifty thousand copies before publication.

CURTIS: Peanuts. Simon and Schuster offered me that for the outline. All I have to do is pick up a phone.

STAGG: *I'll* pick up a phone.

(HE *crosses to phone, starts dialing*)

CURTIS: Who are you calling?

STAGG: What does the phrase "movie sale" mean to you?

CURTIS: Now you're cooking!

STAGG (*Into phone*): Goldie? Mr. Stagg—I'm up in Santa Barbara. I want Hollywood—Hubbub Productions . . . That's right. I want to speak to Harry Hubris personally.

CURTIS: Harry Hubris, the movie mogul? You know *him*?

stagg: We've never met vis-a-vis, Curtis, but in the aristocracy of success, there arc no strangers.

(hubris, *his astonishment at* stagg's *effrontery mingled with admiration, moves downstage and addresses audience*)

hubris: Why, the four-eyed weasel! There goes my plan to steal the manuscript . . . Oh well, I'll just have to buy it.

stagg (*Into phone*): Yes, I'm on . . . Hubbub Productions? This is Emmett Stagg. Put me through to Harry Hubris . . . Harry? Emmett Stagg. How are you, Harry?

hubris: I'm fine—how are you?

stagg (*Into phone, unctuously*): Harry, I've got a book. No, I'm not going to let you read it. I'm just going to tell you one thing. (*Chuckles*) It'll be a tidal wave, and I'm letting you on my surfboard. You've got first crack at the movie rights for three hundred G's!

hubris: Three hundred?

stagg (*Into phone*): Correct, dear heart, but you better talk fast. I've got Otto Preminger on the other phone!

hubris: Two-fifty.

stagg (*Into phone*): Why, you cheap scavenger, you presume to haggle over a symphony?

hubris: Two-seventy-five.

stagg (*Into phone*): Make it two-cighty and we call it *schluss.*

hubris: You got a deal.

STAGG: O.K., Harry—the rest is bookkeeping . . .

> (As HE hangs up and turns, LANCE enters doubled over, the safe in a sling on his back)

LANCE: I've got it, Mr. Hubris! I've got the manuscript, Mr. Hubris!

HUBRIS: Shhh! Shut up—shut up!

STAGG: Who the hell is that?

HUBRIS (Virtuously): I never saw him before in my life!

STAGG: Hubris—? (HE stares at him dumfounded) Why, you low-down crook! Beating me down while all the time you were stealing it!

CURTIS (Wheeling on STAGG): Emmett Stagg, you phony bastard!

HUBRIS (To CURTIS, indignantly): You should talk, you pickpocket! You copped the whole thing from your wife! (Turning on STAGG) And you sold it to me! That makes you a receiver of stolen goods—a fence!

STAGG: I acted in all good faith! He told me he had a novel—

CURTIS (Producing his package): And so I have, right here!

HUBRIS: Then what are we all foompheting about? That's the property I bought! We've got a deal!

STAGG (Turning to CURTIS): By God, we have, haven't we?

LANCE (Puffing, eyes on floor): Is everything all right, Mr. Hubris?

HUBRIS (*Outraged*): How do you mean, all right? We caught you stealing a safe, young man! (*Righteously*) Now, take that box upstairs and clear out while I still have pity on you. (HE *gives* LANCE *a push toward door and latter totters out.* HUBRIS *turns*) Where's the story?

CURTIS (*Hands him package*): Here.

HUBRIS: We're going to make a bundle with this, boys.

GRACE (*Emerging from behind portal*): Oh, no, you won't, gentlemen. All you've got there is a hodgepodge of recipes from *Love and Knishes*.

HUBRIS: Then where is the novel?

GRACE: Right next to your ticker, where it's been reposing all along. Do you want to hand it over, or would you prefer the police to search you?

HUBRIS: Now, look, we're all friends here. Why should we wash our dirty linen in public? (*Points to* STAGG) He's got a contract to publish your book, Mrs. Fingerhead. I got a deal to make a blockbuster out of it. All we need is a topflight screenwriter.

(*Points to* CURTIS)

CURTIS: Gee, thanks, Harry.

GRACE: Well, this has been a most profitable encounter. Shall we adjourn to the rumpus room for a libation on the altar of friendship?

(SHE *motions gaily for them to follow, exits*)

CURTIS: I'll mix you my special long-life gimlet—Somerset Maugham's recipe.

(*Exits after* GRACE)

STAGG: Nothing like a drink when the day's work is done. Join me, Harry?

HUBRIS: Emmett, it's a pleasure to do business with a mom-zer like you. (*As* HE *takes latter's arm to go*) You know, regarding the picture—instead of two-eighty big ones, how about an escalator deal?

STAGG: How do you mean?

HUBRIS: A hundred bucks down and fifty per cent of the Transylvania rights. Matter of fact, you'll make twice the dough that way . . .

(THEY *stroll off,* HUBRIS's *arm draped over* STAGG *in easy cameraderie, and we revolve to—*)

Act II

SCENE 3

SCENE: *Conservatory of the Pasadena estate of* NELSON SMEDLEY, *millionaire founder of the Smedley Snack-eterias. Several exotic plants, an ornamental high-backed Hong Kong rattan chair, a stone bench.*

TIME: *Three days later.*

AT RISE: WORMSER, SMEDLEY'S *private secretary, enters beckoning to* LANCE, *who bears manila envelope under his arm.*

WORMSER (*With oily deference*): Right this way, Mr. Weatherwax, and welcome to Pasadena. Mr. Smedley was so delighted to get your telegram. (*Indicating bench*) Do sit down, won't you?

LANCE: Thank you.

WORMSER (*Winningly*): I don't know *how* our restaurants could function without the Weatherwax All-Weather Garbage Disposal Plan.

LANCE: I'm not here representing the company, Mr. Wormser. It's about a television program I'm planning.

WORMSER: Oh, doesn't matter in the least. Just having you drop in will be such a treat for the Commander. He'll be down as soon as he has his paraffin injection.

LANCE: Golly, is it ever hot in this conservatory. It must be close to 95.

WORMSER: 112, actually, but one gets used to it in time. (*Extracting paper*) Ah, just one trifle—this questionnaire you completed at the lower gate. Now, among your various clubs, you've listed something called the Y.C.L. (*Sudden harsh note*) What does that signify—the Young Communist League?

LANCE: Oh, no, sir—the Yale Camera Lovers. It was my extracurricular activity.

WORMSER: Of course, of course. But you do understand, we can't be too careful with all this subversion around. I'll fetch Mr. Smedley.

(*HE exits. As* LANCE *proceeds to examine plants,* APRIL *enters garbed with extreme, almost Quaker-like simplicity. She carries medicine tray*)

LANCE (*Astonished*): April!

APRIL: Lance Weatherwax! Whatever in the world are you doing here? (*Before* HE *can recover*) The last time I saw you, you were standing in the middle of my living room creating a scene. I've a good mind not even to speak to you.

LANCE: I wasn't to blame for that, April. I tried to explain, but you got me all rattled.

APRIL: And I can see you're still just as confused, dear boy. Why are you staring at me in that extraordinary fashion?

LANCE: Well—uh—you look different somehow.

APRIL (*On the seventh astral plane*): I am different, Lance —as utterly and totally different as can be from the person you used to know.

LANCE: I don't understand.

APRIL (*Infinitely patient, infinitely sweet*): Ah, there's so much you'll never understand, my dear. If I could only bring you to comprehend the change I've undergone . . . Lance, do you know what it's like to come under the influence of a truly dynamic individual?

LANCE (*Still smarting*): You mean that Rob Roy Fruitwell.

APRIL (*With contempt*): That hoodlum—of course not. I mean Nelson Smedley—the founder of Smedley Snacketerias.

LANCE: Well, I know he's a genius in the restaurant game, but what else does he do?

APRIL: He lives life to the fullest. He's vital—uncompromising. He rises above the drab, petty things of life. He inspires every single person around him to serve, to give unstintingly. But of course, you haven't any conception of what I'm talking about, poor boy. You're still the same sweet naïve creature.

LANCE (*With warmth*): Oh, no, I'm not. I had some very rough experiences after I struck out for myself, April. I was pushed around and abused by all kinds of sharpers, like that Harry Hubris . . . but I've learned my lesson.

APRIL (*Patronizingly*): Which is what?

LANCE: To create my own opportunities, to make myself worthy of you, April. I want to earn your respect—to prove myself, so that one day I can claim you.

APRIL: Oh, Lance, Lance, you have so far to go.

LANCE: No, no. (*Taps envelope*) Wait till Mr. Smedley hears the idea I've got in this folder, about the Chocolate Soda Rhapsody. He'll flip, I guarantee you!

APRIL: Now, I hope you're not going to upset him. Mr. Smedley is a very delicately balanced man.

> NELSON SMEDLEY, *supported by* WORMSER, *totters on. He wears a smoking jacket, a skull-cap, is swathed in muffler, shawl and afghan*)

WORMSER: Be careful, Mr. Smedley.

SMEDLEY (*Pulling his arm away*): Keep your paws off me! I can walk as good as the next man—(WORMSER *removes his arm, and* SMEDLEY *falls.* APRIL *and* WORMSER *help him up*) Pushed me again, didn't you? (WORMSER *helps him into his chair*) Who turned off the heat? It's an icebox in here!

WORMSER: It's 118, Mr. Smedley. The putty's melting in the windows.

SMEDLEY: The hell with it. Tell the janitor to put on another coal.

WORMSER: But the boilers are red-hot.

SMEDLEY (*Agitated*): What? What's that about red? Who's red? There's Reds in the house! Reds in the house!

WORMSER: No—no—it's all right. Don't get alarmed . . . April, help me—

(APRIL *and* WORMSER *soothe* SMEDLEY, *lower him back into rattan chair.* SMEDLEY *meanwhile utters peevish whines and grunts like a baby teething.* HE *suddenly catches sight of* LANCE)

SMEDLEY: Who's that? What's he after?

WORMSER: It's the young man who wired you, sir.

SMEDLEY: Did they screen him? (WORMSER *nods*) What's that bulge in his pocket? It's round—it's a hand grenade—

(Ad *libs from* APRIL *and* WORMSER)

LANCE (*Producing orange*): No, sir, it's an orange. I found it on the lawn.

SMEDLEY (*Shrilly*): He tried to steal my orange! Stop thief!

WORMSER (*To* LANCE, *affrightedly*): Look, give it back—quick—

(LANCE *extends it to* SMEDLEY, *who burrows it into his coverings like a chipmunk, chattering his teeth*)

APRIL (*Resentfully, to* LANCE): Now you got him all worked up. Aren't you ashamed?

LANCE: I'm sorry . . .

APRIL (SHE *removes pill from bottle, pours water from carafe, extends both to* SMEDLEY): All right, Commander. Down goes the liver spansule.

SMEDLEY (*Gritting his teeth*): Won't take it! Won't take it!

APRIL: There's a brave little boy.

SMEDLEY: Can't make me. Can't make me!

APRIL: Very well, then, Mr. Stubborn—we won't have our five o'clock romp.

SMEDLEY: I'll take it.
        (HE *spits out pill*)

WORMSER: Now, Commander! (*Maneuvering* LANCE *up to* SMEDLEY) This is Mr. Weatherwax, Commander—you know, the party you consented to see.

SMEDLEY (*Suspiciously*): He looks like the other one—the one that stole my orange. Stop thief! Stop thief!

WORMSER: No, that one went away. This is Milo Weatherwax's son.

SMEDLEY: Milo, eh? We were the same class at Groton. Dirtiest feeder in the school—always covered with oatmeal.

LANCE (*Seeking to ingratiate himself*): My dad often mentions you, Mr. Smedley—

SMEDLEY: Yeah? Well, tell him to give me back that elastic supporter he borrowed. What do you want?

LANCE (*Withdraws place mat from envelope*): Well, I tell you, Mr. Smedley—I've got a sensational idea. I happened to drop into one of your Snacketerias between here and Santa Barbara, and this place mat caught my eye.

SMEDLEY: Hold on! Did you filch that out of one of my restaurants? Stop thief!

(APRIL and WORMSER placate him)

LANCE: Oh, no, sir. I bought it at the souvenir counter.

SMEDLEY: Check on that, Wormser.

LANCE: But the point is—are you familiar with what it says? The text about the chocolate soda? Let me read it to you—

SMEDLEY (Snatching it): I can read, you young squirt. I went to Groton. (As HE starts to read, his hands shake—APRIL and WORMSER steady him. HE clears his throat volcanically) "Hymn to a Chocolate Soda." (Hands shake again. APRIL and WORMSER steady him) What's this? (Returns to place mat) "Arise ye troubadours, and sing a song of nectar. See the great satin ball of mouth-watering mocha, the luscious bubbles whose every secret cell is pledged to arouse—" (Breaks off abruptly) Secret cell? Wormser! Wormser, where are you?

WORMSER: Right here, Commander.

SMEDLEY: Who wrote this Commie propaganda? What's all this about cells? Call John Birch—call John Birch!

WORMSER: I'll have that deleted pronto, sir. Don't you worry.

SMEDLEY (Snarling): Must have been written by one of those wetbacks. Goddam aliens come in and use up all our paper towels! Goddam foreigners—hang 'em all! String 'em up!

APRIL (*Indignantly, to* LANCE): Really, Lance, you deserve to be locked up, raising Mr. Smedley's blood pressure with such nonsense!

LANCE: I wasn't trying to excite him—

SMEDLEY: Shut up, all of you! A man can hardly hear himself read. Now, where was I? You made me lose my place! Oh, here we are. . . . (*Hands shake again—*WORMSER *and* APRIL *steady him*) "Now gird yourself for the climax supreme. Discard the straw, tilt back your head, and treat your tonsils to the celestial ambrosia of flavor, action and chill." (HE *looks up*) Who the devil wrote this?

WORMSER: You did, sir.

SMEDLEY: Well, fire him!

WORMSER: No, you don't understand. You wrote it yourself.

SMEDLEY: Hm-m-m. It's pretty good.

LANCE (*Eagerly*): Do you get it, Mr. Smedley? Do you see it?

SMEDLEY: What?

LANCE: It's a natural—the germ for a sensational TV documentary—a spectacular! "Rhapsody in Bubbles"— an hour program showing the importance of the ice-cream soda in our culture!

SMEDLEY: M-m-m, I don't know . . .

LANCE: Wait till you hear my production plans, Mr. Smedley! Step one—I send a crew to the high Andes to film the life cycle of the cocoa bean—(SMEDLEY *drops gently off to sleep*) Step two—we move a unit into Hershey, Pennsylvania, and live with the syrup as it evolves. (SMEDLEY *falls asleep*) Step three—the marriage of the siphon and the scoop. And mind you—that's only the background for the titles!

WORMSER (*Shakes* SMEDLEY): Commander!

SMEDLEY: Who? What? What's that? Where am I?

APRIL (*Calming him*): It's all right, Mr. Smedley—

SMEDLEY: Get away—I want to hear this. Might just be a possibility . . .

LANCE (*Encouraged*): I haven't even touched the story, sir! We'll plant candid cameras in a drugstore—reproduce an actual soda fountain. For the music I see a really great score—Virgil Thomson—

SMEDLEY: No—no—no—no! That wouldn't sell a lemon phosphate! You haven't thought it through.

LANCE: In what way, Mr. Smedley?

SMEDLEY (*Pontifically*): Now you listen to me, young man —the story of the chocolate soda—harooch!—is the story of Nelson Smedley. You gotta combine the two!

LANCE: By Jiminy, sir, that's a genuinely creative idea! You're dead right!

SMEDLEY: I'm always right! I'll tell you how the thing should be done. The program should open with me sitting on a big banana split, with a large chocolate float on each side. (*To* WORMSER) What d'ye think of that, Wormser?

WORMSER: Commander, you want my honest opinion? The night they televise that, Khrushchev better barricade himself in the Kremlin!

(SMEDLEY *chuckles assent, immediately drops off to sleep again*)

LANCE (*Exultantly*): Boy oh boy, we'll knock 'em cold with that opening, won't we, April?

APRIL (*Loftily*): I really wouldn't know, Mr. Weatherwax.

LANCE (*Wakes up* SMEDLEY): Well, Mr. Smedley, what do you think? Would you sponsor a program like that?

SMEDLEY: Just a minute, young man. I'd have to see a budget on this. The scenery alone could cost a fortune.

LANCE: That's right, Mr. Smedley. We've got to be practical. (SMEDLEY *goes back to sleep*) What we want is an estimate for the entire production. I better get going. (*Turns to* APRIL) April, I may have something pretty definite to say to you the next time we meet. (*Turns back to* SMEDLEY) I'll be reporting back to you shortly, Commander. (*To the trio*) So long for now!

(HE *exits*)

SMEDLEY (*Awakening*): Who's that? What'd he steal?

WORMSER: No, no, sir—that was Lance Weatherwax.

SMEDLEY: Oh, yes, yes—Milo's boy. Seems a pretty bright fella.

APRIL: Yes, you always bring out the best in people, Commander. It's fabulous the way you handle them. You instinctively sense what they want.

SMEDLEY: Damn tootin'. That's why I drew up that document this morning.

APRIL: What document?

SMEDLEY: Tell her, Wormser.

WORMSER: Well, Mr. Smedley felt that inasmuch as you've behaved with such devotion and selflessness, he ought to take cognizance of it.

APRIL: Oh, Nelson, you shouldn't have. Your gratitude is enough reward.

WORMSER: So he's left you his old watch fob—and the rest of his money goes to the fight against Social Security.

APRIL: He WHAT?

SMEDLEY: That's right, honey bun.

APRIL: You're . . . you're joking.

SMEDLEY: Never joke about money, dumpling.

APRIL: Why, you—you—that's the last straw! I sacrificed everything for you—my emotional life, my career, my friends! And for what? (*Her eyes blazing*) I won't remain in this house a moment longer! I wouldn't demean myself!

(SHE *exits outraged*)

SMEDLEY: He-he-he! A clever little minx, but they have to get up early in the morning to pull the wool over Nelson Smedley.

WORMSER: They sure do. (*Glancing at watch*) Well, Commander, it's almost three.

SMEDLEY: Yup—time to watch television. Help me up, Wormser—(*as latter does so*)—and we'll go see who we can blacklist. (HE *shakes off* WORMSER's *hand*) Get your paws off me! I can walk as good as the next man!

    (WORMSER *removes his arm and* SMEDLEY *crashes once again, as we segue into—*)

Act II

SCENE 4

SCENE: A corner of the workshop, the Whirlaway Scenic Studios in Los Angeles. The set contains a litter of flats, lumber, and scenery paint pots. At center, a sculptor's workstand displaying the head of a collie carved from soap; beside it a taboret with chisel, mallet, etc.

TIME: Noon, two days later.

AT RISE: ROWENA INCHCAPE, a matron in her advanced thirties, is engaged in work on the collie's head. She is garbed in a green smock, has an uncompromising henna-colored Dutch bob, wears heavy horn-rimmed spectacles. A short pause, and LANCE enters uncertainly.

LANCE: Pardon me, would this be the Whirlaway Scenic Studios?

ROWENA (Without looking up): It would.

LANCE: They said you build displays for parades and department stores—all kinds of floats—

ROWENA: They hit the bull's-eye.

LANCE: Then this is the place. I'm Lance Weatherwax.

ROWENA: Hallelujah. I'm Rowena Inchcape.

>(SHE *resumes work with her spatula.* LANCE *draws nearer, his interest in her sculpture plainly aroused*)

LANCE: Excuse me. Is that an actual portrait, or more of an idealized conception, like?

ROWENA: Half and half. I based it on our Timmy. He passed over several weeks ago.

LANCE: Oh, I'm sorry.

ROWENA: It was about time, if you ask me. He was twenty-three.

LANCE: You don't say. (*Sympathetically*) Did he die of natural causes?

ROWENA: No, he fell down a well. Nobody's been able to drink out of it since. (SHE *regards* LANCE *steadily for a moment, nods toward sculpture*) Do you like it?

LANCE: Well, you certainly got a good likeness. Of course, I never knew Timmy.

ROWENA: You bet you didn't. If he were alive, you'd never be standing there. He'd have torn you limb from limb.

LANCE: They're great pets, collies. I guess his death was a real loss.

ROWENA: I can't imagine to whom. He bit everybody, right up to the man who chloroformed him.

LANCE: I . . . I understood you to say he fell down a well.

ROWENA: After they chloroformed him. That's how ornery he was. (*Appraising him coolly over her glasses*) But I suppose you're one of those sentimentalists who get mushy about animals.

LANCE: Yes, ma'am—I mean, no, ma'am . . . May I ask what medium you're using there?

ROWENA: Soap—Castile soap. I'm doing it on a Procter & Gamble Fellowship.

LANCE: A head like that must take quite a few bars.

ROWENA: There's enough here to wash a family of fifteen.

LANCE: I always wonder how creative people get started. Were you interested in sculpture from a child?

ROWENA: No, it was an afterthought. I had a joint on Hollywood Boulevard where I eternalized baby shoes.

LANCE: I beg pardon?

ROWENA: Dipped 'em in bronze for ashtrays and souvenirs.

LANCE: But that didn't fulfill you, I guess. The artist is a special case.

ROWENA: The artist is a leech. Scratch any one of 'em and you'll find there's money from home.

LANCE: Ah, that's most interesting. Tell me, which way from here is the float department?

ROWENA: I don't read you, stranger.

LANCE: I'm interested in placing a quite sizable order. I have in mind a banana split approximately eighteen feet long and twelve feet high.

ROWENA (*Eying him fixedly*): How deep?

LANCE: Oh, only about six or eight inches . . .

ROWENA: I see. Do you want nuts on it . . . or just the usual whipped cream?

LANCE: I don't think I've made myself clear. That's only part of it. I also need a chocolate float on each side, maybe—oh, thirty feet high.

ROWENA: Listen, Tom, you're a nice upstanding kid. Why don't you kick that nose candy? There's no future in it.

LANCE: Oh, no, you don't understand. You see, I'm doing this TV spectacular—"Rhapsody in Bubbles"—for Mr. Smedley. You know—of Smedley's Snacketerias.

ROWENA: Look, you're telling me more than I want to know.

LANCE: We have this great opening shot of Mr. Smedley posed against this banana split.

ROWENA: Yeah—yeah. What did you say your name was? Weather what?

LANCE: Wax.

ROWENA: Look, Wax, I only rent studio space here for my work. The party you want is Rukeyser, the foreman of this drop. (*Calling off*) Hey, Virgil! (*With a wave to* LANCE) Well, Tom, nice to talk to you. Good luck with the spec.

(RUKEYSER *enters*)

RUKEYSER: What's up, Rowena?

ROWENA: This civilian's got problems—get out your slide rule. Abba dabba.

(SHE *exits*)

RUKEYSER: O.K., sonny. What's bugging you?

LANCE: Well, I've got a two-float order, Mr. Rukeyser, and I need an estimate for it. I had some rough drawings made to show you. Here—

(HE *spreads them on the floor. As* RUKEYSER *bends down to examine them,* WAGNERIAN, *the studio carpenter, stalks on*)

WAGNERIAN: Now, look here, Rukeyser, I am calling my union.

RUKEYSER: What's the matter, Wagnerian? Isn't the pie finished?

WAGNERIAN: How can I spray on the white of egg until I know if the mechanism works?

RUKEYSER: We're waiting for the broad they ordered for the stag banquet. The clients are coming over for a demo.

WAGNERIAN: She's here. She's been cooling her heels for thirty minutes.

RUKEYSER: Then go tell her to get undressed.

WAGNERIAN: I can't do that! I'm engaged.

RUKEYSER: Do I have to do everything around here? Handle the clients, run after strippers?

WAGNERIAN: Very well! But I'm calling my union.

> (HE *exits.* RUKEYSER *turns back to* LANCE. GODDARD QUAGMEYER, *followed by* SHERRY QUICKLIME, *enters.* HE *is a changed man; his manner is brash and assertive, and sartorially he has become a Hollywood peacock.* SHERRY *is a standard film-colony bimbo*)

QUAGMEYER: Listen, Rukeyser, what's with those blueprints I sent over for the waterfall set?

RUKEYSER: Hiya, Quagmeyer. Didn't you get my message?

LANCE (*Reacting*): Mr. Quagmeyer!

QUAGMEYER (*Waving him aside*): Please, no autographs! We've lost two days' shooting already!

RUKEYSER: I told you, we ran into complications—

QUAGMEYER: For God's sake! An ordinary fifty-foot waterfall with some iridescent rocks!

RUKEYSER: Where the hell do I get the mother-of-pearl for the rainbow?

QUAGMEYER: Call up a button factory—a jewelry-supply house—how do I know? I've got enough aggravation.

RUKEYSER (*Aggrievedly*): And my life is a peach Melba, I suppose!

LANCE: Mr. Quagmeyer—

QUAGMEYER: I told you I was busy, didn't I?

LANCE: Don't you remember me? Weatherwax?

QUAGMEYER: Bubby! What are you doing out here?

LANCE: I'm a director.

QUAGMEYER: It figures. Anything can happen in Tomorrow-land. Look at me. (*To his girl friend*) The last time this joker saw me, I was schmeering my heart out in a New York tenement. I was so hung up on art and all that fakery, I'd have been there yet if it wasn't for him.

LANCE: For me?

QUAGMEYER: That's right! Remember the day you bawled me out—said I had integrity poisoning?

LANCE: Did I say that?

QUAGMEYER: Yeah. That sank home, Weatherwax. I brooded over it all night and finally realized what a fool I was. Yes, sirree, you gave me a whole fresh set of values.

LANCE: But I didn't mean—

QUAGMEYER (*Boisterously*): Who cares what you meant? All I know is I've got a five-year contract at Fox, a white Jag, and the sweetest little head since Helen Twelvetrees.

SHERRY (*Slaps his hand away as* HE *goes to fondle her*): Is this your idea of a fun time, shooting the breeze in a junk shop?

QUAGMEYER: All right, gorgeous, we go toot sweet. (*Smirks at* LANCE) You see? I'm her slave . . . Well, thanks again, fella, be seeing you. If you ever feel like a hot meal, just contact me through my flesh peddler, Monroe Sweetmeat, which he handles Rob Roy Fruitwell and all the biggies.

> (HE *waves, exits with* SHERRY. RUKEYSER *turns back to* LANCE)

RUKEYSER: All right, bud, what's your pleasure? I haven't got all day.

LANCE (*Kneeling by the drawings again*): We need an exact replica of a chocolate float in duplicate, Mr. Rukeyser.

> (WAGNERIAN *and* ELMO *appear, wheeling a large papier-mâché pie, roughly five feet in diameter by twenty inches deep, on a dolly*)

WAGNERIAN (*To* ELMO): Sure, it's heavy. You put a zoftick dame in a deep-dish pie and you've got engineering problems.

RUKEYSER: O.K., Elmo, I'll handle this. (*To* WAGNERIAN) I hope she can breathe in there.

WAGNERIAN: She's in clover. I put in plenty of air holes.

RUKEYSER: I only hope so. Otherwise, we've got a nice little lawsuit on our hands.

(HENNEPIN and POTEAT, *two gentlemen of distinct executive bearing in Homburgs, enter*)

HENNEPIN: Mr. Rukeyser?

RUKEYSER: Speaking.

HENNEPIN: I'm Hennepin of the banquet committee.

POTEAT: And I'm Poteat. You know—the send-off we're giving Floyd Geduldig, our associate in the utilities field.

RUKEYSER: Yep. Well, there's your prop, but let me tell you, brother, it's the last pie I build without specifications.

WAGNERIAN: The whole thing was guesswork.

HENNEPIN: No doubt, no doubt. (*Major Hoople cough*) However, in such a delicate matter, you can't very well expect us to put anything on paper.

POTEAT: The slightest breath of scandal—

RUKEYSER: What's scandalous? You're throwing a feed where a bimbo comes out of a pie and dances with a gorilla. Whose business is that?

HENNEPIN: Ha-ha—quite—of course. (*Inspects pie critically*) Frankly, Mr. Rukeyser, I envisioned something a good deal smaller, with a real biscuit crust.

POTEAT: We were planning to distribute a wedge to everybody after the lady pops out.

RUKEYSER: Biscuit crust? Are you nuts? How would she pop out if she's laying under ninety pounds of dough reinforced with chicken wire?

HENNEPIN: He's got a point, Poteat, it does sound a bit unwieldy. Will this cover of yours lift off readily?

RUKEYSER: Watch (*Calling offstage*) Start the music!

> (HE *presses a button on exterior of pie; the crust jackknifes skyward, and* APRIL MONKHOOD, *clad in the world's scantiest bikini, springs forth*)

APRIL: Whee! (SHE *does a few sinuous steps, climaxing in a bump as* LANCE *gapes at her openmouthed. Then* SHE *turns upstage as a figure clad in super-realistic gorilla costume emerges from behind flat. The latter seizes her in his arms and* THEY *execute short tango routine downstage, at climax of which* GORILLA *bends* APRIL *backward.* APRIL *is carried away, impervious to appeal*) Bombo, you're crushing me in your mighty arms! Release me, Bombo!

RUKEYSER: She's a mental case! Stop the music, stop the music!

LANCE: April!

APRIL (*Blinking as* SHE *regains perspective*): Lance Weatherwax, whatever in the world are you doing here?

HENNEPIN (*Interceding*): O.K.—that's jim-dandy. (*Producing card-case*) Los Angeles Vice Squad. Young lady, you're under arrest for conspiracy to come out of a pie and dance with a gorilla.

APRIL: Why, you rotten, contemptible slobs—

(SHE *turns to flee;* POTEAT *grabs her wrist,* LANCE *springs forward to unhand* APRIL)

LANCE: Let go of her, you!

HENNEPIN: Lay off, punk, or we'll take you along too!

LANCE: You're going to regret this, you wait! That lady's innocent!

POTEAT: Yeah, it's another Dreyfus case. (*Yanks* APRIL'S *wrist*) Come on. You can explain it all to Judge Rinderbrust.

LANCE: Oh, April, how could you ever get involved in such a sordid, awful mess?

APRIL: Don't you criticize me, you mealymouth! I'd never have been here if it wasn't for you!

LANCE: For me?

APRIL: That's right! You rejected me at my darkest hour. I offered you love and understanding—

HENNEPIN (*Impatiently*): Get going—you're breaking my heart.

APRIL (*Hysterically, to* LANCE): Go back to your polo ponies, you rotten little poseur! You're nothing but a dilettante—

a playboy! And you can marry the whole Social Register for all I care! I hate you!

(HENNEPIN *and* POTEAT *drag her off.* LANCE *stands overwhelmed a moment*)

LANCE (*With a groan*): Oh, my god—what kind of a selfish, spoiled brat have I been? Nelson Smedley and his chocolate soda be damned! Television be damned! I've got to save the woman I love!

(*Squaring his jaw,* HE *rushes off, and we segue to—*)

Act II

SCENE 5

SCENE: *A courtroom in the Los Angeles Hall of Justice.*

TIME: *Three days later.*

AT RISE: *A TELEVISION CAMERAMAN pushes on a camera, followed by HANRATTY, a production man.*

CAMERAMAN (*Calling overhead*): Bring it in—push the dimmer up, Voltage! (TO HANRATTY) Where the hell's Judge Rinderbrust? We go on the air at one o'clock sharp.

HANRATTY: He's officiating at a baby derby in Cucamonga. Probably got caught in traffic. But don't worry about Herman J. Rinderbrust. In addition to being the foremost jurist in Southern California, he's all show biz. Kefauver and McClellan pointed the way, but Rinderbrust put the cherry on the parfait. Real-life court cases—living offenders tried before your very eyes!

CAMERAMAN: We go on network at ten A.M., East Coast Time. If we got to throw in *The Mark of Zorro* once more, the agency'll have our heads.

HANRATTY: Rinderbrust'll be here. He's a real trouper.

(JUDGE RINDERBRUST *hurries on clad in his judicial robes*)

JUDGE (*Angrily*): See here, Hanratty, I get a new make-up man by air time tomorrow, or I don't go on!

HANRATTY: I'll call the account exec right after the session, Your Honor.

JUDGE: That flunky! Don't deal with ribbon clerks—call the sponsor direct!

HANRATTY: Yes, sir.

JUDGE: And burn his keyster about that feature story in *TV Guide*. It's cheapening. (*Patting toupee girlishly*) By the way, Hanratty, how do you like the new rug? Mrs. Rinderbrust says it makes me look like David Susskind.

HANRATTY: The women viewers'll eat it up.

JUDGE (*Thoughtfully*): We won't know till the mail starts coming in . . . O. K., what's on the docket?

HANRATTY (*Reads from pad*): Just routine stuff, except for a murder charge and a conspiracy to come out of a pie and dance with a gorilla.

JUDGE: Um—gorilla dancer—not bad. I'll throw the book at her. Should goose the rating. What's the commercial for today?

HANRATTY (*Producing cue-cards*): The usual for Respighi's Bubble Gum—and a new spot for Glo-in-the-Dark Falsies.

JUDGE: Glo-in-the-Dark Falsies? Out, out—I don't plug any product I don't believe in.

(BAILIFF *enters, seats himself below* JUDGE's *bench*)

CAMERAMAN: Thirty seconds to air, and we've got a new advertiser, the Elysian Fields Cemetery Guild in the 1100 block on Lankershim Boulevard.

JUDGE: Cemetery? What are you talking about? I own a row of stores on that block.

HANRATTY: It's the property out back.

JUDGE: Out back is a bog, ten feet under water. A stiff wouldn't last a day in there.

HANRATTY: They're piping the water into fountains, with colored lights. It's a great effect—like Mardi Gras.

JUDGE: Well, that's different. I'll buy it, so long as it's dignified.

CAMERMAN: Judge Rinderbrust! Ten seconds to air! (JUDGE *takes hasty glance at himself in hand mirror* HANRATTY *holds up, skips toward his bench*) Five . . . four . . . three . . . two . . . one . . . whoof!

JUDGE (*Into camera*): Good morning, fellow citizens, and welcome to "The Scales of Justice," the only program that brings you real lawbreakers, malefactors and hoodlums—people like yourselves in a peck of trouble. Yours truly, Judge Herman J. Rinderbrust starring! (*Raps gavel*) All right, bring on the first culprit.

BAILIFF: The people of the State of California, the County of Los Angeles, versus Miss Roxana DeVilbiss.

(A POLICEMAN *leads on* ROXANA, *a shapely miss clad in very revealing nurse's uniform*)

JUDGE (*Licking his lips*): Well. And what's the charge against this little transgressor?

BAILIFF: Operating an unlicensed massage parlor.

JUDGE (*Regards* ROXANA's *garb intently*): So you're a massoose, are you? My, what a lovely turtle-neck sweater.

ROXANA (*Indignant hauteur*): Your Honor, this is a miscarriage of justice! I'm a respectable college grad—the Slenderola Body Institute in San Berdoo.

JUDGE (*Peering deep into her bodice*): This court has a very warm feeling toward San Berdoo. They raise the largest casabas in the West.

ROXANA: Thank you, Judge. Now, me and my colleagues at the Idle Hour Massage Parlor perform a very important role in the community.

JUDGE: You restore men's souls as well as their bodies—right?

ROXANA: Exactly! By what we call psycho-massage.

JUDGE (*Emotionally*): You nurse your fellow man back to health, you bring roses to his cheeks.

ROXANA: Oh, definitely, Judge!

JUDGE: In short, you rediscovered the Fountain of Youth.

ROXANA: Yes!

JUDGE (*Angrily*): And for this those lousy Puritans—those keyhole peepers—seek to penalize you? (*Turns majestically into camera*) Ladies and gentlemen of the TV audience, I want you to look upon this tiny defendant, and I want you to remember another frail little person without a license—viz., and to wit, Florence Nightingale. (*Rising*) As long as I wear these judicial robes, the sovereign state of California will remain a haven and a refuge for all healers of the feminine gender, with and without certificates! Case dismissed.

ROXANA: Gee, Herman, you've been a peach.

JUDGE: I'll look in on your store to see that my orders are carried out.

ROXANA: I'll tell the girls.

BAILIFF (*As* ROXANA *exits*): The People of the State of California, the County of Los Angeles, versus Joe Gourielli, alias the Truth Swami, Haroun Azeez.

(GOURIELLI *enters, clad in turban and business suit*)

JUDGE (*Examining his charge sheet*): Swami, you're charged with creating a public disturbance. On the night of the 24th, at the intersection of La Paloma and Alta Yenta, you did willfully stage a human sacrifice. Think fast, Gourielli.

SWAMI: The sacrifice, yes—the disturbance, no. The Apostles got overheated and started to grab souvenirs from the funeral pyre.

JUDGE (*Outraged*): Who do you think you are, knocking off citizens like they're clay pigeons!

SWAMI: They're followers!

JUDGE: Makes no difference! This is America, Gourielli! Everybody's entitled to four square meals, a second car, and the right to croak when he sees fit—not when some wog sets fire to him. This is an extremely grave offense.

HANRATTY (*Anxiously, with papers*): Judge, just a minute. (*Into camera*) Ladies and gentlemen, while the Judge is pondering the facts of the case, we pause briefly for station identification. (*To* JUDGE) Don't be too tough on him, Judge. Remember our new sponsor, the Elysian Fields Cemetery Guild.

JUDGE: By Jove, you're right! We mustn't discourage business. This zombie is good for forty plots a week. Give me a close-up. (*Into camera*) Ladies and gentlemen, on due consideration, everybody's entitled to religious freedom and to a fine, decent funeral at reasonable prices. If you have a loved one who has recently given up the ghost, insure their future through the Elysian Fields Cemetery Guild. Make their journey to the Happy Hunting Grounds a memorable experience for relatives and cadaver alike. (*Carried away,* HE *starts to sing "Dear Old Girl"—stops himself*) All right, Gourielli, back to your devotions but keep your nose clean.

BAILIFF: Miss April Monkhood. Charged with conspiracy to come out of a pie and dance with a gorilla.

(APRIL *has entered, clad in virginal, subdebutante-style coat*)

JUDGE: Ah, the Gorilla Dancer! (*Into camera*) Televison viewers, once in every jurist's career, he is confronted by a case so shocking that the mind reels. The one you are about to witness surpasses anything in my vast experience. The culprit did knowingly plot and agree with accomplices unknown to emerge from a pastry and engage in a lascivious dance with an anthropoid. Behavior like this would have the most dubious effect on young American womanhood, and I, as its legal guardian, intend to squelch it root, branch, lock, stock and barrel. (*To* APRIL) Now, then, young woman, what do you have to say for yourself?

APRIL: I was tricked, Your Honor. They claimed it was an experiment—

JUDGE: None of your shilly-shally. How do you plead—guilty or not?

(A *hubbub offstage, from which emerge voices of* POLICEMAN *and* LANCE *as latter struggles to enter*)

POLICEMAN: Stand back there, you!

LANCE: I'm involved in this case, I tell you! Let me in!

JUDGE: Who's that? What does he want?

LANCE (*Struggling*): Judge Rinderbrust—please! I've got to talk to you!

JUDGE (*Beckoning*): Come up here. (*Severely*) Look here, you, you're in a court of law. What do you mean, creating this uproar?

LANCE: I want to testify for the defendant, Your Honor!

JUDGE: Have you got any new evidence?

LANCE (*Emotionally*): Your Honor, you're making a terrible mistake! This lady's innocent—I've known her for years. She's a distinguished artist—a cultivated, refined person—

JUDGE: Don't waste my time with character references! Produce your evidence!

LANCE: I saw the performance, Judge—there was nothing offensive in it! She did a little dance—

JUDGE (*Raps his gavel—rises majestically*): Now you listen to me, young fellow. The law explicitly states, *ex parte* and *nolens-volens*, that he who comes into court with clean hands is *sub judice* prejudiced *a priori*. In other words, "*Exceptio probat regulam de rebus non exceptis.*" Once and for all, before I pronounce sentence on the accused—have you any evidence relevant and germane to this case?

LANCE (*Produces an envelope*): I have, Your Honor.

JUDGE: Hand it to the clerk of the court. (LANCE *gives envelope to* BAILIFF) But I warn you, there are no extenuating circumstances in this case. O.K., what does it say?

BAILIFF (*Takes envelope, extracts check, reads*): "Pay to the order of Herman J. Rinderbrust five hundred thousand dollars. Signed, Octavia Weatherwax."

JUDGE (*Thwacking gavel*): Case dismissed!
    (APRIL *and* LANCE *react joyfully, dissolve into embrace. As* JUDGE RINDERBRUST *raises his hands in benediction over them, a couple of* PRESS PHOTOGRAPHERS *run on, blaze away at the couple with flashbulbs as we segue into—*)

Act II

SCENE 6

TIME: One month later.

SCENE: The WEATHERWAX library.

AT RISE: APRIL, a bride's headdress and veil surmounting her head, stands arm-in-arm with LANCE, both their faces set in the strained grimace of the conventional society wedding photograph. The two PRESS PHOTOGRAPHERS crouch at opposite angles, aiming their cameras. OCTAVIA fidgets impatiently nearby. In background, MRS. LAFCADIO MIFFLIN, a majestic dowager well-boned over the diaphragm, with avian headgear and a froth of ruching at her throat, alertly observes the tableau.

FIRST PHOTOGRAPHER: Hold it!

SECOND PHOTOGRAPHER: O.K., now—personality! Just one more!

(Their flashbulbs explode. OCTAVIA steps between them)

OCTAVIA (Imperiously): All right, gentlemen, that's quite sufficient. You've held up the wedding rehearsal long enough. (*As* PHOTOGRAPHERS *exit*) Run along, children, I'll be with you directly.

(LANCE *and* APRIL *go out,* MRS. MIFFLIN *joins* OCTAVIA)

MRS. MIFFLIN: Octavia, love, your daughter-in-law couldn't be more captivating.

OCTAVIA: Oh, Milo and I are enraptured with her.

MRS. MIFFLIN: And so well bred for a theatrical person.

OCTAVIA (*Tinkly little laugh*): My dear, that phase of April's was just puppy fat. Started way back when she was a senior in Miss Hewitt's Classes.

MRS. MIFFLIN: I thought you said she was at Foxcroft.

OCTAVIA (*Adroitly*): Both, darling—you know how volatile these girls are nowadays. Well, her mother was determined to send her to Bryn Mawr, of course—family tradition—

MRS. MIFFLIN: Was that Alicia Monkhood who captained the field hockey there in Tucky's year?

OCTAVIA: Oh, no, this was the Scottish branch. They derive from Llewellyn Fitzpoultice, ninth Viscount Zeugma.

MRS. MIFFLIN (*Nodding*): Of course. That's where she gets that fair English skin.

OCTAVIA: And her willfulness, dear child. Nothing would do but she must run off and join Martha Graham's troupe, and when Lance saw her at Jacob's Pillow, he naturally fell head.

MRS. MIFFLIN (*Pouting*): Wretch. I still think you might have shared the secret with your eldest friend.

OCTAVIA (*Hurried kiss, maneuvering her off*): You'd have spread it all over Prout's Neck, you know you would.

MRS. MIFFLIN: Shall we see you at the Dingbats' Thursday?

OCTAVIA: No, I believe Milo's tied up that night at the Luxor Baths.

MRS. MIFFLIN: Well, tell him how happy we are for the both of you. (*Fluting as SHE exits*) Goodbye—ee—ee . . .

(LANCE and APRIL reappear, his demeanor clearly rebellious)

LANCE: Gosh, Mater, do we have to go through all this mumbo-jumbo?

OCTAVIA: Indeed you must, and you may as well put a good face on it.

LANCE: But the things that really matter are spiritual—aren't they, April dearest?

APRIL (*Guardedly*): Well . . .

OCTAVIA: Lance, darling, you talk like a sausage. The things that matter are objects one can touch—viz. and to wit, diamonds and furs and blue-chip securities. Only we on the distaff side understand that.

APRIL: You sure are cooking on the front burner. I may be horribly naïve, but blindfolded in a London fog I can tell mink from stone marten, and it's all thanks to you, Mother Weatherwax.

OCTAVIA (*Graciously*): I like your spirit, April. My first reaction when our son brought you home to our stylish Park Avenue triplex was that you were a cheap little tramp. Nothing you've done since has caused me to alter that opinion.

APRIL: Thank you, Mother Weatherwax.

OCTAVIA: But what can be keeping Milo?

LANCE: What Milo is that?

OCTAVIA: Why, your father, which he is probably handling the management reins of our far-flung interests.

MILO (*Entering briskly*): Wrong as per usual, my pet. A young protegée of mine, a geology student, was showing me some rare stones over at Cartier's.

OCTAVIA (*Acidly*): And you totally forgot the surprise we are giving Lance.

MILO: Applesauce. The relevant documents repose inside this very envelope. (*Extracts one from breast pocket*) Lance, I hope your creative Odyssey has taught you something.

LANCE: It did, sir. I found there's an awful lot of prejudice against money. Especially from people that don't have any.

MILO: They should be machine-gunned.

OCTAVIA: Hear, hear!

APRIL: You can say that again.

MILO: I will. They should be machine-gunned. (*To* LANCE) But paradoxically, Lance, you also have a responsibility to them.

LANCE: I don't dig you, Guv.

MILO: It's up to you to stamp out that prejudice tooth and nail. (*Handing him envelope*) My boy, I've set up a mighty foundation in your name—tax free—to bring culture into every American home.

LANCE (*Glowing*): Gee, Dads, me—the final arbiter of truth and beauty!

MILO: You may meet resistance to your concept of what's clean and straight and fine, but if you do, just cram it down their throats.

LANCE: Will do, Dad!

MILO: But remember that in this weary old world, there's one value that transcends all others.

(ROXANA DE VILBISS, *in nurse's uniform, enters bearing fancy baby basket trailing swaddling clothes.* SHE *passes it to* LANCE, *who transfers it to* MILO)

OCTAVIA: Why, Milo, there's a suspicious moisture in your eye.

MILO: Yes, I'll 'fess up to same, hardened cynic though I am. (*Clears throat*) Friends, this little bundle of happiness is everybody's joy. We must cherish it—share it with us, won't you?

(As HE tilts basket forward, revealing it crammed with greenbacks, HE dips into it, starts showering it over the audience like a farmer sprinkling grain)

CURTAIN